Word Up:
THE LIFE OF AMANDA GORMAN

NY Times Best-seller
MARC SHAPIRO

For more information contact:
Riverdale Avenue Books
5676 Riverdale Avenue
Riverdale, NY 10471

www.riverdaleavebooks.com

Design by www.formatting4U.com
Cover by Scott Carpenter

Digital ISBN: 9781626015906

Trade Print ISBN: 9781626015913

Hardcover ISBN: 9781626015920

First Edition July 2021

This book is dedicated to…
All the women
With the power
To be smart
To grow
To prosper
To dig down deep
And to do
What has to be done
I have such women in my life
My wife Nancy
My daughter Rachael
My granddaughter Lily
My agent Lori
They have what it takes
To make life what it is
And to make it right

Table of Contents

Author's Notes
Time Has Come Today

Why a book on Amanda Gorman? A more logical question might be why not? Or how about this. Why now? Well into 2021, all questions seem relevant.

There's no denying it: Donald Trump's presidency and the last four years may be behind us, but the division he's caused and the discourses his presidency has forced us to have has left the country divided and wondering, "where do we go from here?"

People are angry, choosing up sides and demanding the truth. The only problem is, they don't know who to turn to. In a world filled with an ever-changing culture and political landscape, the people need a stern, emotional voice to propel them forward, to give them hope, and, most importantly, to give them not only the hope to envision a better tomorrow, but the hope to create a better tomorrow. But let's be real, this is 2021, when paper-thin entertainers and prefab pop stars and their hollow words just aren't cutting it anymore. People need substance, something that'll last just a bit longer than the ever-shifting scroll that is social media. And still we hold out hope for something better—solid ground—if you will.

In comes Amanda Gorman, a talented only 23

year-old Black woman who is a passionately fresh voice who seems to have come out of nowhere who will take the fight to the streets and to the people and be a guiding light in the darkness. She is of the moment, the here, now and all the small in-betweens that make life worth living.

The genesis of this book was simple. I saw, along with the rest of the world, Amanda Gorman reading "The Hill We Climb" at the presidential inauguration. I saw the potential of something socially and historically important. In my mind, it made me remember the emergence of social conscious in the 60's, when right was might and Martin Luther King, John Lewis and The Freedom Riders were on the land. In the best possible way there were shivers down my spine.

I called my agent. She said, "Do it!" There was little to debate. It was a story that was all too perfect not to tell. It was a go.

Word Up: The Life of Amanda Gorman was a rarity for me. Positive, inspiring, hopeful, all that good stuff. I've been at this a long time, exploring the lives of people, the good, the bad and the ugly. I've never been one for cynicism but I've always been leery and ever-vigilant of the people I write about, no matter what kind of version of them I have in my mind. If there was a blemish to be found, a fault to be explored, a not quite so pure and angelic moment in Amanda Gorman's life, I would have found it. But at the end of the day, there was not a moment in chronicling Amanda Gorman's journey so far that I doubted the honesty and sincerity of Amanda's spirit, her goals and the challenges she faced and overcame.

In its own way, this book would be easy and it

would also be hard. The facts are the facts. Names, dates and places are set in stone. Adding nuance and depth would be a whole other matter. Requests for interviews and insights into Amanda's life and times were either never acknowledged or some variation of "sorry" or "I can't talk to anybody without Amanda's permission." Fair enough, I thought. Fortunately, for the purposes of research, there was a time when not only Amanda, but the very same people who were not talking now were talking freely then, which helped fill in the blanks when it came to things like character and philosophy.

As the book evolved, *Word Up: The Life of Amanda Gorman* started to become something more than a young adult-oriented bio with an intended youth target audience. As I unfolded the pages of her journey, I watched as small subtle moments and calculated choices of ambition and passion changed her from a child, to a child with a dream, to finally somebody on the verge of adulthood and great success, who sprouted into a successful poet with a promising future. It was in that moment I realized Amanda Gorman's journey and her emerging success wasn't just another generic tale of achievement, but the latest link in the chain of proud Black women writers who have taken up the pen to battle an unjust system They too would need to be acknowledged.

One element of Amanda's personality that would be a constant throughout her life, was the methodical nature of how she went about achieving her goals. She would see a challenge, and then sit down and figure out what she had to do to overcome it. There were never any fits of temper or depression or anguish. Amanda always seemed to, logically, have it all together. Even when there were difficulties or problems, by the time it was made public, which was not often, it was only to disclose that the problem was solved.

Watching her life unfold and the persistence and drive that marked her path was a joy to behold. In these truly cynical times, it was a pleasure to come to the conclusion that nice people can finish first with their integrity, morality and character intact.

And in the process bring the concept of words put together on the wings of passion as a mighty sword; words with the power to make the world think, feel and have hope that the drive for peace and harmony is truly not a lost art.

Word Up: The Life of Amanda Gorman is not by any means the end of the road. There are many more worlds for Amanda to conquer. This book is only the first step.

Marc Shapiro
Summer, 2021

Preface
March 5: Amanda as a Threat

Amanda Gorman knew the things she wrote about were out there.

She had found out about reality from the newspapers, television, talking about people who had been there and done that and she had heard all the tales told around the urban campfire of a big city. Amanda's source material had been everyday life, a reality that being Black made it almost impossible to avoid.

She had written about the fear and dread almost constantly in her poems, but angst and defiance was always there, holding up a literary mirror to her worldview and the idea of what was right and wrong. Amanda's words spoke the language of what it was like to be Black, or any other marginalized person living in a world where simply walking down the street could result in looks that were often ringed with derision and suspicion.

But truth be known, Amanda had never really experienced the rough, raw racist backhand of society up close and in person as a child. She had been brought up in a polite, sedate and academically isolated world in multicultural California.

Years later, she was making her life in the public

eye, surrounded by celebrities, politicians and international figures of stature and prominence. She had been effectively insulated from the everyday pressures of being other than white.

But all that was about to change.

On March 5, 2021, Amanda Gorman was coming home after a long day of being in the spotlight at a youth-focused poetry event. She was in good spirits, a feeling of accomplishment surrounded her like a halo. But as she approached her apartment complex, a different kind of reality confronted her.

Amanda had realized that a security guard had been following her for some time. She was suddenly unsure of the situation. What could she have possibly done to draw this attention? As she neared the entrance to the apartment, the security guard approached her. "He demanded to know if I lived there because I looked suspicious," Amanda later related her experience in a tweet chronicling the incident.

There were some tense moments. Amanda was not used to abrupt interrogation in her world.

After Amanda showed him her keys and buzzed herself into the building, Amanda recalled that "he left. No Apology."

After the incident, Amanda was angry and defiant. "This is the reality of Black girls," She wrote later on in her tweet. "One day you're called an icon, the next day a threat. In a sense, he was right. I am a threat to injustice, to inequality, to ignorance. Anyone who speaks the truth and walks with hope is an obvious and fatal danger to the powers that be. A threat and proud."

Amanda Gorman now had her own tales to tell.

Introduction
Amanda Meets World

Amanda Gorman turned 19 on March 7, 2017.

It would be a very good year, a year in which a lot had happened to someone who was admittedly amazed by it all.

"Oh, I am 19," she told *Vice Magazine*. "Sometimes I feel like Cicely Tyson in a 19 year-old body because I forget that I'm 19."

Amanda had been a well-kept secret for some years in the world of literature, poetry and academia. A poetry protégé with a definite social and activist bent, she was well on the way to notoriety by the time she turned 14.

And light years away from those days when she was trying hard to discover just who and what Amanda was all about.

In 2014, Amanda was chosen the first *Youth Poet Laureate of Los Angeles* on the strength of poetry that *Urban Word* writing nonprofit organization executive director Michael Cirelli once described in a *KCET* story as "timely, earnest and sincere." Her drive to literally spread the word for young poets resulted in her starting her own nonprofit writing organization called *One Pen One Page*. At an extremely young age, Amanda was a regular on the Los Angeles poetry circuit, giving regular readings at schools, museums and bookstores. And later, while carrying a full freshman class load at Harvard, she also became a published author with the *Urban World* release of her first collection of poetry, *The One For Whom Food is Not Enough*. All of which she accomplished at the ripe old age of 16.

But for Amanda, 2017 would be the watershed year, a year when her talent and persistence would burst upon the mainstream. In 2017 Amanda was named the first *National Poet Youth Laureate* and would subsequently read at the opening of the literary season for the prestigious *Library of Congress*. A July 4th celebration saw Amanda reading her work backed by the legendary *Boston Pops Orchestra*. It would be a busy time for Amanda as she juggled formal education with the responsibilities of being the *National Poet Youth Laureate*.

"I went on this tour around the US," she told *Rolling Stone*. "It was just me in a lot of meetings in rooms and museums, trying to learn as much as possible."

And what Amanda discovered was that she had grown quite easily into a role model on a national stage. "I've been doing a lot of traveling and speaking to young people," she explained in a *Vice* conversation. "I've been having meetings with a lot of educators and administrators. I enjoy doing interviews because it's an opportunity for me to speak about issues that I'm passionate about—education, equality and environment."

September 2017 would mark a coming out of sorts for Amanda. Tracy K. King, a poet of much emotion and power, was being honored for her selection as *Poet*

Laureate of The United States. It was a triumphant moment for the arts set against the backdrop of the *Library of Congress*. It would be a personal acknowledgement for Amanda when she was asked to read as part of the inauguration ceremony for Tracy K. King. In an excerpt from a conversation with the *Library of Congress.com*, Amanda recalled that she was a bundle of nerves as she made her way from a day in class from Harvard to Washington D.C. for the event.

"I tore out of my sociology research class and took the stairs two at a time. I had a few minutes to get back to my dorm, grab my suitcase and head to the airport for D.C. My hands shook with excitement and nausea. I still couldn't believe it. I was ready to board my flight."

Once at the event, minutes flew by. Meeting with notables in the academic and literary world and with Tracy King were magic moments for the young Amanda, the equivalent of meeting a favorite pop star. Before she knew it, Amanda was ready to take center stage.

"My heart is always dancing in my throat before I perform," she said in her *Library of Congress.com* conversation. "This time it felt like a grenade waiting to explode."

Amanda took the opportunity to unveil "In This Place: An American Lyric," a powerful homage to this life and these times that began this way:

> There's a poem in this place
> In the foothills, in the halls
> In the quiet beat of the seats
> It is here, at the curtain of the day
> Where America writes a lyric

She would recall in the *Harvard Crimson* how she was a literal bundle of nerves as she finished her reading. "My knees were shaking. I was so stressed and done by the end of it I just went backstage and took my shoes off. Then I was called back on stage and I came out barefooted."

"In This Place: An American Lyric" was a powerfully big step into the public eye and a strong statement of life and times changing and coming of age. As Amanda would acknowledge in an interview with the *Harvard Independent*, it was a creation with far-reaching intent. "I wanted it to feel like an American poem, meaning that it was something that could be understood from a wide array of cultures and also a wide array of geopolitical moments."

The response to "In This Place: An American Lyric" was both unexpected and universally and critically applauded. The emotionally moving ode to tragedy, bravery and hope, set against the backdrop of an American landscape stark and not always bright, was picked up and critically praised in all manner of media.

Eventually, the reading and Amanda's poem caught the attention of Dr. Jill Biden, a teacher and, given the moment, more importantly the wife of the recently elected *President of the United States* Joe Biden. The previous four years had been tumultuous, with social and political factions and views colliding in a downward cycle of corruption, lies and dishonesty. Biden had used the theme of unity rather than division to capture the presidency and was looking to his inaugural ceremony to play on that theme. But it had not been quite that simple.

After four disheartening and dispiriting years of

Donald Trump and the Republican Party's draconian leadership, the campaign and the election had been a politically bloody one, full of lies and gutter politics from the far right that only served to further divide the country. The Democrats won. The Republican's lost and there were more than enough truly visible scars to go around. The specters of racism, police brutality, blatant corruption and dishonesty had driven a seemingly irreparable wedge through the country. It was an unsteady time on the land to say the least and a true civil war seemed a strong possibility.

And it was in the midst of this political and spiritual quagmire that Amanda received an unexpected phone call.

Dr. Biden had seen a video of Amanda's performance of "In This Place: An American Lyric" and felt she would be the perfect element of the inauguration to play up her husband's positive hopes for the country. It would be mid-December 2020 when Amanda received a phone call from the Democratic Inauguration Committee, inviting her to read as part of this pivotal moment in American history.

"There was a lot of screaming and dancing around my apartment when I got that call," she recalled in a *PBS News Hour* interview. And then there was a lot of questioning and no small amount of doubt as she related on the *Late Night with James Cordon* talk show. "I'm 22 and I've overcome a speech impediment. Who would want me onstage? Then they called and offered me the opportunity and I danced around in my socks like a crazy person."

Once her excitement passed, Amanda set about writing, in early January 2021, the original piece of work that would be "The Hill We Climb." The Democratic Inauguration Committee would give Amanda relatively free reign in writing the poem but, as she would recall in an *Associated Press* interview, there were a few buts. "I was encouraged to highlight the ideas of unity and hope and it was recommended that I stay away from anything that might sound like I was celebrating the end of Donald Trump's presidency."

But those "suggestions" were be minor in contrast to the joy and freedom that being a part of history this opportunity was offering "They did not want to put guardrails on me at all," she told *The New York Times*. "The theme for the inauguration was '*America United.*' When I heard that was their vision, that made it easy for me to say 'great!' That's also what I wanted to write about."

But even with all the excitement and joy of this opportunity, there was also doubt and a hint of fear. "I had not been expecting that at 22," she offered *ABC News*, "that they would trust me with such an honor. At that moment, I was honestly scared of writing such a poem. I wasn't sure that I could even do it justice."

But, thinking very much like a poet of the times, Amanda saw the challenge as equal parts creative and philosophical, to be both personal and political. A true poet of witness. "You're speaking for everyone but you also don't want to speak for everyone," she told *PBS News Hour*. "I knew I wanted the poem to be both robust and accessible. It was really a difficult dance to do."

Not surprisingly, Amanda went to work right after receiving the inaugural invitation. Like a true scholar of the arts, she began reading the works of previous inaugural poets as well as such historically important orators as Abraham Lincoln, Frederick Douglass and Winston Churchill to get a feeling for the way they went about delivering the emotion and the message of their work. Amanda knew she was the new kid on the poetry scene and was not taking any chances. All eyes would be on her, so she knew she had to get it right.

And those early doubts were balanced out by her adulation of another inauguration poet, Maya Angelou. Amanda had not only found inspiration in Maya Angelou and her accomplishments but also her challenges as well. Like Amanda Gorman, the legendary poet had dealt with speech issues through much of her life. Angelou's biography *I Know Why the Caged Bird Sings* and her inauguration poem were works Amanda often turned to for inspiration in many of her earlier poems. And so, in Amanda's challenge to craft her own inauguration poem, Amanda once again turned to Angelou for support and inspiration.

"I grounded myself with her inauguration poem 'On the Pulse of Morning,' she acknowledged in a recent interview with Oprah Winfrey. "It was an amazing discovery when I was reading *I Know Why the Caged Bird Sings*. In trying to write a poem worthy of inauguration, I would constantly listen to Angelou's poem 'On the Pulse of Morning' for inspiration," a poem that Angelou wrote for President Clinton's inauguration in 1993.

Amanda would struggle during the writing of "The Hill We Climb," often spending agonizing days that only resulted in a few lines. "I had this huge thing, probably one of the most important things I'll ever do in my career," she told *The New York Times*. "It was like if I tried to climb this mountain all at once, I was just going to pass out."

Amanda worked on the poem nonstop for a week and was about halfway through when, on January 6, 2021, fate, in the form of a violent insurrection and assault by insurrectionists, stepped in to guide Amanda and "The Hill We Climb." Amanda said to *PBS News Hour,* "I was about halfway through writing the poem when we had the insurrection at the Capitol. I don't want to say that my poem took a drastic left turn at that point but those events just solidified for me how important it was to have a poem about unity and a new chapter in America."

Amanda had found the emotional crossroads of hope, fear, struggle and the good fight, as she told *The Los Angeles Times*. "When I saw the insurrection at the Capitol, that was the day the poem really came to life and I really put the pedal to the metal." She would be adamant in telling *The New York Post,* "That day gave me a second wave of energy to finish the poem."

And in finding the missing emotional link to "The Hill We Climb," she knew she would have to face some uncomfortable truths. "America is messy," she told *The Los Angeles Times*. "It's still in its early development of all it has become and I couldn't ignore that. The poem had to recognize these scars and these wounds."

As she put her words on the page of "The Hill We Climb," she felt she had found the poem's importance and meaning for these days and times she was living through post-insurrection. "My hope is that my poem will represent a moment of unity for our country and, with my words, I'll be able to speak to a new chapter and a new era for our nation," she explained to *The Washington Post*.

In the days leading up to the inauguration, Amanda garnered an increase in media and public interest that went beyond the accepted norms of poets and poetry at such a young age and so early in a writing career. Her notoriety had grown at such a pace the previous year that she signed an unheard of two-book deal with the mainstream publisher *Viking*. With the announcement of her participation in the inauguration, pre-sales for all her books (which at that moment had not yet been scheduled for publication) were quickly slotted for April and September of 2021 and immediately went through the roof. Her already loaded interview schedule had increased ten-fold.

That was the good stuff. But with the good stuff came the pressure.

"When I first wrote the poem, I was thinking that in the week leading up to the inauguration I would be rehearsing every day," she told *Time Magazine*. "But everything was moving so quickly I actually did not sit down with the text until the night before. There was a lot of nights before performing in the mirror."

Amanda was about to make history as the youngest poet to read at a presidential inauguration in the history of the United States. The challenge of reading her poetry in front of literally millions in person and through countless media outlets brought up the question of how her long-standing childhood speech impediment, which, like President Biden, she had dealt with and overcome, would stand up to the rigors of the moment.

Amanda was very human and very young and so

there would be those last-minute moments of very normal anxiety as the day arrived. When she saw the White House grounds done up in larger-than-life decorum and the crowds began to gather, she would recall those final moments of nervousness and doubt as she stepped to the podium. In her televised conversation with James Corden, host of the *Late Night with James Corden* talk show, she shared her thoughts from that day, "I'm cold. I know Biden is right behind me. How does my hair look? My nose is sniffling. Don't trip."

The world was about to find out.

On January 20, 2021, amidst the glitz, glamour, pomp and pageantry of the moment, Amanda stepped to the microphone, looked out over the vast expanse of people and things that made Washington D.C. a magic kingdom, flashed a bright half impish/half nervous smile and began to read "The Hill We Climb":

> When day comes we ask ourselves
>
> Where can we find light in this never-ending shade?
>
> The loss we carry,
>
> A sea we must wade.
>
> We've braved the belly of the beast
>
> We've learned that quiet isn't always peace,
>
> and the norms and nations of what just is
>
> Isn't always justice.

"I showed up at the podium and I laid it on the floor," Amanda later recalled to Oprah Winfrey. "I knew the poem was written and all that was left was for me to embody it and I was going to do that to the best of my ability."

Amanda completed her reading of "The Hill We Climb" to thundering applause from the assembled dignitaries and celebrities. She looked out over the expanse of the Capitol steps and was emotionally overwhelmed. After making her way from the podium, and being congratulated by the likes of Barack and Michelle Obama and singer Lady Gaga, Amanda, with her mother in tow, retreated backstage where, as she recalled in *People*, it all began to sink in. "Afterward my mom and I were just real quiet backstage. We knew our world had changed in six minutes."

The impact of that six-minute reading would be instantaneous.

Congratulations from the likes of Oprah Winfrey, Lin Manuel Miranda, Michelle Obama and others from the United States and around the world were streaming in. *Time Magazine* put Amanda on the cover of their February issue which featured a one-on-one interview conducted by Michelle Obama. Presales of all her books shot to number one on the Amazon charts months before their actual publication date. A special collectors' edition of "The Hill We Climb," with a foreword by Oprah Winfrey was rushed together to capitalize on the moment and was published on March 30.

The big names and the big television shows were falling all over themselves for an interview or even a few brief moments of her time. The mania for all things Amanda was off at a gallop and coming in torrents. The prestigious *IMG Models* signed Amanda to a fashion, beauty and talent endorsement deal.

Amanda the poet was now celebrity royalty and it seemed like everybody on the planet was acknowledging her talent and her power to do great and mighty things.

It would have been easy for Amanda to fall prey to the hype machine that was now cooking on all cylinders. For somebody so young and so into poetry and the literary life, this was a strange new world to encounter and deal with. But it would be to Amanda's credit and down to earth nature that she was able to see through all the noise and, as she would acknowledge on the television show *CBS This Morning*, keep her eye, metaphorically speaking, on the prize.

"One of the preparations that I always do whenever I perform is to say a mantra to myself which is 'I am the daughter of Black writers. We're descendants from freedom fighters who broke through the chains and changed the world. They call me.' That's the way I prepare for the duty that needs to be done."

Chapter One
Born This Way

Amanda and her twin sister Gabrielle were born 45 seconds apart on March 7, 1998. Which of the two twins came first was never verified and in hindsight was of little importance. What was important to their single mother, Joan Wicks, was the fact that her daughters were premature births and, according to doctors, were born quite healthy.

Except for their last name, the identity of their father has rarely been acknowledged, even in passing and, by all accounts, their biological father has never been in his children's lives. But in an interview with *Cultural Weekly.com*, Amanda indicated that not having a father in her life was impactful.

"The divorce of my parents is not something that I remember but the rupture and the chaos it caused afterwards, right when you're born into the world, and to be born into that dysfunctional and chasm-filled family, I think that presented itself many moments of sadness and sometimes joy, but also a lot of pain. That was just a big deal."

Fortunately, their mother more than compensated for the lack of a father figure. Wicks, a schoolteacher, highly educated, motivated and socially and racially aware and whose family had a history of being creatively oriented was more than equipped to raise her children the right way. Wicks was determined to give her children, which included an older son named Spencer, every chance in the world to be something and somebody.

Amanda's earliest memories were of a tiny, serviceable apartment in the Southern California city of Westchester, in an area that was growing socially and racially. "Growing up, I was surrounded by so many colors and so many tongues," she explained to *The Los Angeles Times*. She would be more poetic in her memories of that time when talking to *The New York Times*. "I grew up in this incredibly odd intersection in Los Angeles. It felt like Black hood met black elegance met white gentrification met Latin culture met wetlands."

Life in the Gorman household in those early years was geared toward achievement and education. And Wicks was quick to lay down the ground rules. She kept the television off because she wanted her children to grow up engaged and active. When they were allowed to watch, it was primarily safe and sanitized 50's and 60's sitcoms like *The Munsters* and *The Honeymooners*, so old that they were shot in black and white. But even those rare occasions came with a condition as Amanda recalled in the *Harvard Crimson*. "If I wanted to watch regular television, I would have to make a social justice argument to my mother as to why I should be able to."

While the television rules and regulations made perfect sense to the Gorman girls, Amanda recalled in *GirlBoss.com* that it took a bit of explaining when their friends were around the house. "Whenever my friends came over, they were like 'Why is your television screen in black and white?' And I was like 'What are you talking about? Isn't this what everyone's screen is like?' "

Although Amanda and her sister were, perhaps, too young to grasp the significance of the rules and regulations their mother was teaching them in those formative years, Amanda years later in conversation with *Ten Magazine*, acknowledged that there was a method to her mother's attitude toward child rearing. "My mother gave her all to influencing the hearts and minds of a rising generation."

Amanda and her sister took easily to their mother's brand of child rearing that was equal parts love and encouragement. In an interview with *Time*, Amanda recalled that she and her sister Gabrielle had it pretty well. "As twins, we were actually pretty dissimilar but what bonded us was our personalities and our values. We were raised by a strong Black woman who taught us to value our ideas and our voices."

Gorman's memories of those days were vivid as she offered *The Los Angeles Times*. "We made forts, put on plays and musicals. And I wrote like crazy."

To the point where Amanda's mother would have to turn to bribery in order to get a good night's sleep. "My mom used to pay me quarters every day I stayed in bed instead of waking up super early to write and waking her up," she revealed to *The Coven Magazine.com*.

Amanda's grandmother, Bertha Gaffney Gorman, had a front row seat to her grand children's earliest creative efforts as she recalled in a *Real Black*

3

Grandmother's.com interview. "When they would come for the summer or visit for vacations that was our entertainment. They would write, they would make a play and they would perform it. It was just part of what we did. The kids were very creative."

Admittedly, those early writing efforts were a child's first tentative step but Amanda's mother always encouraged the efforts as well as gently guiding her toward the importance and love of reading. "I've been writing poetry ever since I can remember," she explained to *National Public Radio*. "I was maybe four or five. It wasn't good at all. But having an arena in which I could express my thoughts freely was just so liberating."

Amanda would tell *Study Breaks.com* that those early childhood days and her mother's emphasis on education made an immediate impact. "Having a mother being a sixth grade English teacher in an inner city public school gave me an up close and personal view of how literacy influences young students. I realized early on that education can really be a life or death experience. I saw it as a pathway to get off the streets and to break a cycle."

Of course, there was more to Amanda's upbringing than formal education. Wicks made it clear from the beginning that running a household as a single mother had its own challenges and that every member of the family would have to pitch in with the chores. It was something that Amanda and her siblings easily adapted to and brought to their lives a strong sense of humility and responsibility. "I've never had any reason to get a big head in my family," Amanda said in an interview with *Ten Magazine*. "If my room's not clean, I dare not leave it. My mother made it very clear that there was no such thing as a get out of jail free card."

But behind her mother's intent to make a good life full of opportunities for her children, Wicks was ever vigilant and concerned that the premature nature of their birth might have an impact on her development. Wicks would address her concern in a conversation with *Understood. Org.* "Amanda was inquisitive and a bit of an overachiever. She had trouble expressing herself but she was always advanced in her thought."

Wicks' concerns were confirmed when, just before entering kindergarten at age five, Amanda was given a series of tests and was diagnosed with *Auditory Processing Disorder* and speech articulation issues that would see Amanda struggle with comprehension and the inability to pronounce certain letters, most noticeably the letter R. Wicks immediately sensed the challenges Amanda would face in the coming years but it was a philosophical, positive stance that led Amanda's mother to believe that everything was going to be alright.

"Every child has a gift," she told *Ten*. "It just has to be discovered."

Amanda got the message, acknowledging in a *Harvard Gazette* interview years later that her perceived drawbacks were anything but. "I always saw it as a strength because since I was experiencing these obstacles in terms of my auditory and vocal skills, I would become very good at reading and writing."

And by the time Amanda reached five, she was already making that all-important decision on how to meet her challenges head on and to overcome them.

"The voice I was reading on the page was the voice I really wanted for myself," she explained to *The Harvard Gazette*. And in the same interview she was quick to lay those early discoveries at the feet of her mother. "While my mom is not a poet, she has definitely inspired me in so many ways. She is a big piece of who I am."

Chapter Two
New Roads and *Dandelion Wine*

The distance between Westchester, CA and Santa Monica, CA was 13 miles one way, approximately 15 minutes.

It was a journey Amanda and her sister Gabrielle would make twice a day, five days a week for the next 13 years. Their destination would be a private, alternative school named New Roads School. And the mere act of travelling through the city would, in later years, prove to be a mighty influence on Amanda.

"I was exposed to different cultures and backgrounds early on," Amanda told *Study Breaks.com.* "From Little Ethiopia to Chinatown, to Santa Monica Beach, to downtown Los Angeles. I paid witness to a cornucopia of identities."

Wicks had sensed from the beginning that her daughters, and especially Amanda, would benefit from a more non-traditional education and had managed to get both of her girls into the school on scholarships. New Roads School's project-based learning approach to progressive education was well-balanced and tailored to a no grades curriculum that made learning facts and information important but not most important, instead encouraging its students—a cross section of races, genders and socioeconomic circumstances—to create individual goals from their lessons and to discover how they would use that information in their own lives.

Amanda now often praises New Roads as a driving influence in her life choices, as witness conversations with *California Charter Schools Association.org* and *Bucknellian.net*. "We were expected to take what we were learning and put that information into action. From the beginning, I was motivated to think about my own knowledge and learning."

Amanda's early years in New Roads were balanced out with therapy designed to help her deal with her speech challenges. In a sense, she was setting herself up, even in a liberal setting like New Roads, to be considered 'different.' But Amanda's mother was not going to let that happen. She arranged for Amanda to receive 'accommodations' (tools designed to help those with disabilities keep up with the rest of their class).

Initially, the already headstrong young girl was not thrilled with the idea of being helped. "I'm so stubborn," she told *Understood.org*. "I refused to use the accommodations. But my mom pushed me to use 'the extra time' on my tests. My challenges just for me were something that was a reality. But I knew I had strengths too, especially when it came to reading and writing."

But all the confidence in the world did not stop Amanda from thinking of herself, despite an outgoing nature that allowed her to cultivate a circle of friends, as a bit of an outsider. "Looking back in elementary school, I often described myself as a plain, weird child," she admitted to *The New York Times*. "I spent most of my elementary school years convinced I was an alien. While other students were on the jungle gym, I was writing in a journal on a park bench or trying to write my own dictionary. I was obsessed with everything and anything. I wanted to learn everything, to read everything, to do everything. I was constantly on sensory overload. I'd hoard dozens of books in my second grade cubby and literally try to read two at a time, side by side."

During this period, Amanda showed a wide-ranging attitude toward reading. Although she would acknowledge that she had a preference for the likes of *Harry Potter* and *Jane Eyre*, but was quick to acknowledge in *The Bucknellian.net* that "I loved reading everything I could get my hands on. I would read and reread books until they were falling apart in my hands."

But as Amanda would explain to *The Argonaut*, her creative instincts, in those early years, was still in a state of flux. "I always really liked to tell stories and I did that before I knew that was writing. I'd get pieces of notebook paper and draw pictures and maybe a few lines. I just thought 'Hey, this is my head. This could be cool.'"

Amanda would continue to benefit from her mother's positive feedback and encouragement of just about everything her young mind could create. That daily, positive energy from her mother would become a consistency in Amanda's life that would always push her forward. Amanda would describe the typical interaction years later in conversation with *Black Enterprise Magazine*. "I was showing my mom some of the work that I had been doing. I had been painting and doing visual art over my poetry and she was like 'This is really something. You should keep on this path.'"

Amanda's mother constantly encouraged her daughters to stretch, creatively, in any and all possible directions, all the while couching their experiences in the reality that sometimes they would win and sometimes come out not quite good enough. It was years later during a 2017 story telling session put on by the New York organization called *The Moth,* and held at the Cutler Majestic Theater in Boston, when her mother encouraged her to go to a Los Angeles audition with more than 100 child actors for the role of Nala in a Broadway version of *The Lion King.* Recalling that experience during *The Moth* appearance was an exercise in storytelling, humor and the art of the literary style put down.

"The air smelled of Hollywood and desperation," she recalled. "It was crammed with these monster mothers and their savage children. You have no idea. These kids are like little demons. They'll step their foot out to trip you. They'll be doing pirouettes around just to show off. Randomly just do a back flip because they can."

Amanda would fail the audition but, in hindsight, was not the least bit disappointed. "Part of me was so glad to know that I would never be like one of those girls who made it to Broadway because I would still make it here. I'd still make it to now, being loud and proud in front of a crowd."

Amanda was slowly but surely finding her way. Her speech challenges coupled with the earliest rounds of therapy often made her a bit of an oddity to her classmates who often mistook her speaking pattern as that of somebody from another country, often mistaking her for a British or Nigerian immigrant.

For Amanda it would all be good fun as she would acknowledge at various points in the *Harvard Gazette* and *People.* "It kind of became a mini experiment. If they thought I came from Europe, they would treat me very well. It was like I was sophisticated or an intellectual. I remember being asked from a young age 'Where are you from?' and 'You talk funny.' People were so insistent on trying to pin down why I was so different from them."

But children of that age were quick to gloss over Amanda's disabilities in favor of her welcoming personality and positive outlook. She was a little different, but it was a different that appealed to them. Her reading and, by degrees, writing skills were evolving but she was still very shy about the concept of reading and performing in front of an audience.

That would change during the second grade when Amanda took a big step forward when, during class one day, she performed a monologue in the voice of an Indian Chief named Oceola. Amanda recalled the moment with *The Los Angeles Times.* "I'm sure anyone who saw it was aghast at this 15-pound Black girl who was pretending to die on stage as a Native American Chief. That moment was important in my development because I really wanted to do justice to it and bring it to life."

Amanda's third grade year would offer up inspiration to enter another level of creation. New Roads teacher Shelly Fredman would regularly read books to the class that she felt would inspire them to think and achieve. Amanda would recall vividly to *The New York Times* the day her horizons were broadened when Shelly Fredman read the class the book *Dandelion Wine* by noted science fiction writer Ray Bradbury. Amanda was immediately struck by the poetic nature of Bradbury's words. "I'll never forget being in third grade and my teacher Shelly Fredman read *Dandelion Wine* to our class. I lost my mind. It was the best thing I'd ever heard. It was pure magic."

It was clear to Amanda that Bradbury's words had struck her creative soul, as she would tell *The Argonaut*. "That was so magical to me. All his metaphors. All his characters. I was so blown away that I started reading and writing a lot after that. It really took off."

The Bradbury book had transfixed and transformed Amanda. Writing was suddenly something that she just had to do. And it was not long after hearing *Dandelion Wine* that Amanda would sit down and write her very first poem and, although the title has long since left her memory, what drove her to write it was clear.

"I was an extremely sad third grader," she recalled to *Culture Magazine*. "Very cute but very sad. The interesting thing about it was that I knew I was sad and depressed. The way I dealt with it was to write." Amanda would further elaborate on her first attempts at writing poetry years later when she told the *Sacramento Observer*, "I had a lot of untitled poems I wrote in the third grade and a lot of those were about feeling like the black sheep of the herd."

Amanda was fortunate to have encouragement from the faculty of her school during those early days of writing. Poetry fragments were treated as fully formed poems and she was encouraged by her teachers to keep her creatively and emotionally on the right track.

"Thanks to my teacher Shelly Fredman, I began to respect myself as a writer and a poet," she offered *The Project for Women.org*. "She encouraged me to keep writing even if I was off topic and man, I was off topic every time. She made sure I felt valued as a writer. It was in that class that I wrote my first set of poems which covered how alone and strange I felt. I wasn't part of the clique at my school. I got along better with my teachers than I did with students my age. I didn't feel like being a cerebral, daydreaming to the point of danger, skinny Black girl with a speech impediment was helping my popularity. But I found power in writing about being outside the in crowd."

Third grade would end up being a pivotal time for Amanda. She was finding her voice amid a myriad of challenges that most third graders were not having to deal with. For an eight-year-old.

"I think it was about not having friends," she reflected in *The Argonaut*. "I had friends in the third grade but, for some reason, I felt very isolated because I was into reading and writing and I really cared about what was going on in the world. A lot of third graders weren't like that so I was literally the black sheep in the herd. So I felt kind of in my own little bubble in that grade.

"So I wrote a poem about that."

Chapter Three
Write On

Although Amanda had seemingly found her calling at age eight, her calling came with the distractions and contradictions of childhood and the fact that, by her own estimation, she was quite the peculiar child.

"I always felt like the strange kid and the odd man out," she remarked to *The Project for Women*. "I liked sitting and pondering the sunset and digging up fake fossils. I knew I wanted to do something creative when I got older. I taught myself watercolors and a few chords on piano and guitar."

Amanda readily acknowledged in conversation with the *Lily blog* that, beginning around age five, music was her primary focus. "I wanted to be a songwriter. I thought that was going to be my thing. And I definitely went through my own emo phase. But I finally realized that I could not sing to save my life."

Eventually Amanda realized her early song-writing efforts had a structure and cadence that seemed very much like poetry and storytelling and so she began to move away from sound and music to words on a page. At the encouragement of her teacher Fredman, Amanda began writing actual poetry. Much of Amanda's earliest efforts at poetry were either forgotten or thrown away, but Amanda always remembered there was reportedly a sense of passion, power, determination and an eye toward activism and feminism in her early works.

But while she was encouraged by her New Roads teachers to keep at it, there was always the shadow of her speech impediment lingering over her efforts. "The letter R is the bane of my human existence," she would tell *The Harvard Gazette*. How much of an anchor her speech challenges would be was brought out during a wide-ranging interview with *National Public Radio*. "In one poem I wanted to say 'Girls can change the world.' But I could not say so many letters in that statement so I'd say things like 'Young women can shape the globe.'"

Nevertheless, any doubts she had were easily overruled by the sheer awareness, power and intensity that Amanda was finding in her poetry at such a young age. Those in the New Roads faculty who had been aware of her growing prowess as a very young poet, teachers who had read her earliest work, were already hoping that by the time Amanda reached their grade level, they would have her in their class.

By the time Amanda reached the sixth grade, the now 10-year-old was brimming with a quiet confidence as only a child with a lot of promise can. On the website *Inspiremykids.com*, it would be reported that Amanda was already telling anyone who would listen that she was going to be *President of The United States* one day and that she was driven to use her words to transform the world for good.

Nobody who knew Amanda could doubt her.

But before Amanda could work on a presidential

future, her mother sought to expand her knowledge in a much more well-rounded, religious context. And for Wicks, that meant becoming parishioners at the *St. Brigid Catholic Church*, long established as a South-Central Los Angeles church that emphasized both traditional and progressive thinking. And it was in this community that Wicks hoped to expose her daughters to the Catholic faith that was relevant to their identity as African Americans.

St. Brigid would welcome Wicks and her daughters with open arms according to parishioner and former director of religious education Floy Hawkins in conversation with *Religion News Service*. "Their mother was very intentional about her girls. That was very clear and, as a result, the girls were very responsive to the African American worship experience. One could tell from the beginning that they were a very humble family. They're a family that loves to share but are not imposing people."

During their middle school years, Amanda and Gabrielle attended the church's religious education program and would stay with the curriculum through their Baptism, First Communion and Confirmation. Hawkins would recall that Amanda, in particular, was progressing as a poet with the confidence to stand up in front of a congregation and let her voice be heard. "Amanda would participate in the church's Black history program and would recite her poetry."

And even in the halls of God, Amanda's words would often be greeted with applause and a standing ovation.

Chapter Four
Speak Easy

After finding her creative muse in poetry at age eight, Amanda would spend the next seven years, in a literal sense, voiceless. When it came to putting words and emotions to paper, she was unmatched in her intensity, and in her drive to touch people and bring them into her world, she was light years ahead. But when offered that all-important step in her evolution as a creative being to go public, she would instinctively shrink back into the shadows.

Amanda was afraid to step before a live audience and read out loud. It was a fear that she had been carrying around for some time. "As someone with a speech impediment there is always a concern," she admitted to *Time*. "Is the way I'm saying it, good enough? My last name is Gorman and I could not say it until about three years ago."

Amanda would grow to acknowledge the stumbling block that would frustrate her growing talent as a poet. By the time she turned 14, Amanda was determined to break the cycle of frustration that was brought on by her speech impediment. "I had a speech impediment and so I couldn't use my voice," she told *CBS This Morning*. "And so I arrived at the point in my life in high school where I said, 'You know what? Writing my poems on the page isn't enough for me. I have to give them breath and life. I have to perform them as I am.'"

To deal with her impediment, Amanda, organically, developed a psychological and logical pattern of fusing her writing skills with auditory outside influences, namely her love of music. She would break down how she made the transition in a conversation with *CNN*.

"I used writing as a self-expression to get my word on the page but, then, it also metamorphosized into its own pathology. The more that I recited out loud, the more in which I practiced spoken word, the more I was able to teach myself how to pronounce those letters which, for so long, had been my greatest impediment."

She would acknowledge in the same *CNN* interview that the letter R continued to be a major stumbling block and that she would turn to a favorite piece of music, a song from the soundtrack of the Broadway musical *Hamilton*.

"I would listen to the song 'Aaron Burr Sir' from the Broadway musical *Hamilton,* which is just packed with R's, and I would try to keep up with Leslie Odom [the singer] as he is doing this amazing rap. I told myself 'if I can keep up with that rap then I can train myself to say the letter R'." Amanda would emphasize the importance of rap in her breakthrough in a conversation with *Open Studio with Jared Bowen*. "If I can rap, if I can do those poetics at that speed, and with those intonations, that was helping me to figure out how to say those sounds."

Wicks was encouraged by her daughter's willingness to deal with her obstacles and the progress she was making in mastering the written word and, by the time her daughters turned 14, was searching for every opportunity for them to nurture their talents. Amanda's writing and Gabrielle's growing aptitude in a cinematic sensibility were a constant joy to Wicks who was now convinced that the potential in her daughters' future was endless.

"Where there's a deficit, there is a place where the child can make it up," she told *The Sun* when exploring her confidence in Amanda's ability to overcome her speech impediment. Always someone who preferred to stay in the background, in a rare interview with *The Los Angeles Layolan*, she took a bit of credit for what her children, and especially Amanda, had accomplished during the early part of their lives. "Amanda started writing like our rent depended on it when she was seven years old. When people ask how she became a good writer, I tell them it was nothing but hard work and practice. And I think it made them better students because mom was very dedicated to school."

Wicks would find the ideal adjunct to her daughter's creative leanings when she discovered a group called *Write Girl*, a nonprofit organization founded in 2001 by former singer/songwriter Keren Taylor with the intent of helping teenage girls be all they could be by nurturing their creative potential. The Los Angeles based writing and mentoring organization seeks to promote creativity, critical thinking and leadership skills through writing workshops centered around various forms of writing and one-on-one mentorships with seasoned writers.

Amanda and Gabrielle would pass the requirements to join *Write Girl*. But Assistant Director Allison Deegan was more than a little unsure about their prospects after meeting the two girls for the first time. "They were tiny and looked much younger than their years," Deegan recalled in conversation with *USC Annenberg Media.com*. "You just wondered what you were going to see from people of this stature."

Deegan was also initially concerned about the baggage Amanda brought to the table, her continued speech impediment and the speech therapy she was taking. But Amanda's presence in *Write Girl* soon became a high point of the group's workshops on the days she presented her work. Deegan recalled the excitement on the days when the "mighty words" would come out of Amanda's mouth and the "double takes" people would do when they heard the diminutive girl recite her work. "It was always clear, literally from day one, that she had a lot to say, that her poetry was about large-scale themes, appropriate for everyone and that she was really intent on using her poetry to share really important messages," she reflected in *USC Annenberg Media.com*."

Amanda's progress during her early days at *Write Girl* was steady. It was known during those early days that Amanda was attempting to write a novel and was also dabbling in short stories. But Deegan was quick to clarify to *USC Annenberg Media.com* that Amanda was quickly finding her niche as a poet. "I don't mean to say that she didn't write other things. But she defined herself as a written poet and a performative poet early on. You could see the cadence, you could see the hand movements. You could see the presence on the stage as she matured and grew into it. That poetry was her thing."

Deegan was not alone in her assessment of Amanda. Writing mentor Michelle Chahine Sinno worked with Amanda during that time and would meet weekly with the young girl, usually at a Los Angeles café where they would work through writing prompts. One day, Sinno suggested that Amanda write about her view from the café where they were sitting. "When she was reading to me what she saw, I was amazed," she recalled to *LA List.com*. "This was just a city sidewalk but the way she saw the world was amazing."

At that time, Amanda considered herself more of a fiction writer and continued to say that she was working on a novel, quite a feat in and of itself for a girl so young. "I actually never thought I'd do poetry as a career," Amanda told the *Harvard Advocate*. "I started out writing short stories and fiction and thought those were going to be the things that I did."

But Sinno would soon determine where Amanda's true talents lay. "She'd come to me with pages and pages that, interestingly, were filled with poetry but she might not have known it."

While Amanda was progressing creatively, her mother made sure she was aware of the reality of being Black in America. At a fairly young age, Amanda's mother sat her down and read her her Miranda Rights, a series of questions and/or statements read to somebody by the police either for criminal or an interrogation situation. Her mother's not very subtle tutorial would make an immediate impact on the young girl.

"When you are a Black child growing up in America, our parents have to have what's called 'the talk' with us," she told *The Washington Post*. "Except it's not about the birds and the bees and our changing bodies. It's about the potential destruction of our bodies. My mom wanted to make sure I was prepared to grow up with Black skin in America. That was my first awakening to the potential climate I was stepping into."

And it would be this awareness of the reality of being Black in America that would have an impact on Amanda's writing as she would acknowledge in conversation with *Cultural Weekly*. For a girl barely 15, she seemed wise and mature beyond her years. "I see myself as an activist who manifests her passion through art. Being a girl in this world… who that is and reaching out and observing the world and being brave enough to confront that and then moving past that into how I see the world now is how I'm approaching what I do."

Write Girl encouraged Amanda to take the next step, to overcome the self-consciousness of her speech impediment and read her poetry before an audience. For Amanda, it was her very first reading in a *Write Girl* workshop that broke the barrier and, as Amanda recalled in an excerpt from an essay Amanda contributed to *The Huffington Post*, it was a moment of doubt.

"I mounted the stage to read my poetry at a writing workshop, thinking why did I even volunteer to read my work? More than being nervous about the quality of my poem, I felt anxious about what my voice would sound like. Would the audience understand me? Would they wonder what foreign, exotic country I came from? Would I have to tell them that my accent was not an accent but a disability? I clutched my journal tighter in my sweat drenched palms and prayed my clumsiness would not emerge, causing me to trip on my two left feet. As I stood, I experienced a sudden gratitude for the blinding lights. I could not see everyone's faces! That made things much easier. I opened my book and began to read."

Amanda's breakthrough performance was a first step and a small step. As her confidence rose, she would feel more comfortable in workshop readings and the tentative first steps into a more public arena. She was beginning to feel the rush as her creativity entered a new, more public, phase. And as her poetry transformed, so did Amanda. But she was quick to point out during a *National Public Radio* interview that her challenges were always there.

"I would be in the bathroom, five minutes before (a reading), trying to figure out if I could say 'Earth' or if I could say 'girl' or if I could say 'poetry.' And you know, just doing the best with the poem that I could."

Chapter Five
One Giant Step

Amanda's coming out as a poet who not only read her work but performed it as well was a liberating experience for the poet. However, it was not so much a sudden burst as it was a gradual evolution that Amanda has always couched in organic terms as she explored in conversation with *National Public Radio*. "I'm not sure if it was so much a proactive choice as it was kind of answering a calling. It [reading her poetry] kind of just started happening more and more. That was the last place I expected anyone to want me. But, as I continued to write and share my poetry, I became brave enough to read at cafes and things like that. I started to get invited to read at occasions and I would say yes."

Along with Amanda's readings at the café and through every opportunity present through *Write Girl*, the poet also did readings at bookstores and even the occasional poetry competitions. Among those early poetry competitions were appearances at the prestigious *Beyond Baroque* readings. Those privy to those early appearances must have sensed a true talent on the rise, rough and occasionally tentative but always forthright, powerful and challenging. That she had emerged as a poet of the printed page and challenging message was a given. That she was now able to get her words across in a live setting was the proverbial icing on the cake.

But ever the perfectionist, Amanda was on a seemingly never-ending journey to improve on her chosen craft. To her way of thinking, there always seemed to be something that could be improved upon or taken in a different direction.

Creatively, Amanda would reach a crossroads while a sophomore at *New Roads School* when her voracious reading habits crossed paths with a noted African American author, Toni Morrison.

"In the eighth grade, I picked up Toni Morrison's book *The Bluest Eye* because I had never seen a book with a dark-skinned, nappy-haired girl on the cover," she recalled in an interview with *Race/Relations* newsletter. "I was enthralled not just by Morrison's craftsmanship but also by the content of her stories and her characters. It was then that I realized that all the stories I read or wrote featured white or light-skinned characters. I had been reading books without Black heroines which nearly stripped me of my ability to write in my own voice. Reading Morrison was almost like re-teaching myself how to write unapologetically in a Black and feminist aesthetic that was my own."

The education and, for that matter, the re-education of Amanda as she learned about Black literature, continued to be guided by a close circle of family and schoolteachers. In a conversation with *Rolling Stone*, Amanda would recall one sage bit of advice. "I once had a high school teacher tell me that I should not let school get in the way of my education."

Amanda would take that bit of advice to heart in 2013. She had become more attuned to activism and feminism in all its forms, reading voraciously on all subjects with a racial and social agenda and looking for every opportunity to ply her creative and philosophical skills in those arenas, especially given that her schooling didn't provide her with such a nuanced education at her age. She became particularly inspired on the occasion of watching a United Nations speech by Pakistani Nobel Prize Laureate Malala Yousafzai, a young activist for the rights and education for women who had often risked her own personal safety by her activism. Amanda was struck by Malala's youth and determination and set out to do what she could do to help further the cause.

In a Tweet, Amanda would chronicle what happened next. "Watching a video of Malala at the UN, I gave myself one year to join the cause at the UN in any way I could."

Amanda looked into the idea of going public with such thoughts and was thrilled when her efforts resulted in her being selected as a *United Nations Youth Delegate* to the 2014 *Commission on the Status of Women* held at United Nations headquarters in New York. Amanda would be both wide-eyed and determined as she ventured into the cavernous confines of the Big Apple. Wide-eyed at the sights and sounds that enveloped her. Determined to meet the movers and shakers at the United Nations and to have her voice heard.

According to a delegate report in *United Nations Association.org*, Amanda was literally the star of the Commission proceedings. Far from a shrinking violet in the face of this gathering of countless countries, Amanda was conspicuous in raising her voice to diplomats and UN representatives with probing questions about the rights of women in the world. At one point, firing off with determination "How do we reverse the trend of feminism as an elitist issue? We should be focusing on integrating it with primary school curriculums but, instead, gender equality programs are proliferating at universities."

For Amanda, her UN experience would be a mixed bag. She would make her mark as a young woman of drive, determination and substance. But she would also acknowledge the disappointment she experienced in an interview with *Study Breaks.com*. "I went to the UN as a youth delegate and was not being taken seriously. Many of the panel moderators at the UN *Commission on the Status of Women* would make well-meaning but, simultaneous, patronizing comments about my age."

But rather than take offense at the sly remarks directed against her because of her youth, the ever-resourceful Amanda, in conversation with *Girl Boss.com*, used the perceived put down to her advantage. "It got to the point that, if I was emailing people or contacting people, I would not tell them my age or my high school. I tried to leave that information out as much as possible. Then I would sit down at these meetings and people would see me and be like 'Oh she looks 12.' But it can work in my favor when people see what is being done and they realize that it is such a young person doing it."

Amanda's reputation grew with her confidence, but it would still be a cautious coming out with gradual steps. Even while Amanda was wowing her audience with the power and message of her words coming from such a young voice, she was still unsure of how speaking in public with the occasionally still pronounced speech impediment was resonating with the outside world. It would be an insecurity that would come to the fore in Amanda's mind when, in 2014, when it was announced that Los Angeles, spearheaded by the organizations *Urban World LA* and the *LA Arts and Athletic Alliance*, would be making history by establishing the title of *Los Angeles's First Youth Poet Laureate*.

Now a sophomore at New Roads School, and with the encouragement of her mother and the community of teachers and mentors, Amanda, with more than a touch of reluctance, applied for the position. "I thought they won't want me because I drop my R's," she would recall in an interview with *Cultural Weekly.org*. "What if people don't understand me? So, I was like 'should I apply?' I was very nervous and I was sure I wouldn't get it because of the way my voice sounded."

Amanda's insecurities went beyond her speech issues to her tendency to be her own toughest critic as she would relate in an interview with *TLA Magazine*. "I didn't necessarily consider myself that strong of a poet. But I was glad to see that the role [of Poet Laureate] included a commitment to social justice, service and community change, all of which were important to me. So I sent in poetry, a video of myself performing and my resume."

Amanda was up against the talents of more than 150 young writers. Amanda and the other finalists would read on June 14 at the *Los Angeles Central Library* in a packed *Taper Auditorium*. Amanda gave a powerful reading and remained anxious and nervous as she awaited the judge's final decision, declaring Amanda the winner. "I felt really touched that the judges were able to see that I did have a soul and a spirit despite the way that I sounded," she told *Cultural Weekly.com*.

The notoriety and accolades surrounding her selection grew in the coming months as Amanda made a number of public appearances and readings and did a number of interviews in which she deftly answered a number of literary, creative and philosophical questions with ease. The consensus among observers of the Los Angeles scene was that Amanda would, most certainly, singlehandedly lead the reemergence of Los Angeles as a poetry center of the world. Amanda was fully aware of these proclamations and the notion that she was now thrust into the center of it. And she took on this responsibility with ease, youthful confidence and no small sense of style and grace. All the while continuing some sense of normalcy as a student at New Roads School.

It would be during those early days of going public with her poetry that Amanda would make the acquaintance of noted poet and author Dinah Berland who would mentor the young girl for a number of years. Berland would recall the day the two met in an interview with *Warren-Wilson.edu* that she was in the audience the day Amanda was reading at the Museum of Contemporary Art in Los Angeles. "Amanda got up there and she was so far superior to the other kids. I wanted her to know that she was special so I followed her out of the museum and found Amanda sitting alone on a bench."

Amanda accepted Berland's compliments and that was seemingly the end of that. Until a representative from *Write Girl* contacted Berland and said they had the ideal young girl for her to work with. It would turn out to be Amanda. They would meet regularly at local coffee shops around town and discuss and read numerous poets. Amanda would also read her latest work. Berland would turn out to be the ideal sounding board for Amanda who, Berland recalled in *Warren-Wilson.edu*, was very serious about learning everything she could about her chosen craft. "Amanda wanted to understand everything about how poets became poets."

Into 2015, Amanda decided that it was time to take the next step in her evolution as a poet by publishing her first book. More of a DIY/self-published collection of poems which would ultimately see the light with Penmanship Books, *The One for Whom Food is Not Enough*, (currently out of print), was met with critical praise from many corners, with reviewers falling all over themselves in praise of a young girl with a powerful voice.

No lesser light than famed poet and poet laureate Luis J. Rodriguez summed up the large embrace of *The One for Whom Food is Not Enough* when he offered, "Amanda Gorman draws from deep wells, of ancestors, community, suffering souls, vibrant women, hungry youth and the unmined gold of language."

Amanda felt her first book was largely autobiographical and straight to the point as she explained to *Cultural Weekly*. "It's just really my narrative, being a girl in this world and who that is, and also reaching out and observing the world. It's about starting with my origins and being brave enough to confront that and then moving past that to how I see the world."

But as she related in an essay for *Vital Voices.org*, what to do with the sudden notoriety as Los Angeles' First Youth Poet Laureate and the promise of her first published book was a bit daunting. "I was an 80-pound sophomore who had just been named the Inaugural Youth Poet Laureate of Los Angeles. I was nervously trying to figure out what I wanted to do with my platform to promote literacy. I didn't even understand taxes, let alone how to start an organization."

It was then that Amanda crossed paths with *Her Lead,* a national organization made up of influential women and industries who provided fellowships, including financial and mentorship support as well as guidance, to the next generation of young women leaders. Amanda knew she needed the kind of insight and support *Her Lead* could offer and so she applied for a fellowship. In short order she was accepted. Amanda was thrilled at the positive response and the invitation to fly to Washington D.C. to take part in an introductory meet and greet and to present her ideas to the organization. In due course, Amanda and her mother were on their way to Los Angeles International Airport and a flight to Washington D.C. for a meeting whose outcome could only be measured in Amanda and her mother's hopes and dreams.

Amanda would recall in *Vital Voices.org* the emotional moment when they arrived at the airport and the impact of what was about to happen came bubbling out. "My mom got all teary eyed when we got to the LAX terminal. We could both tell that this would be an exciting new chapter for me."

Amanda was like a girl in the proverbial toy store as she took in the sights and sounds of the big city. Her enthusiasm for the city would only be upstaged by the experience of meeting influential women as well as young girls like herself, all dreaming the same dreams and looking for somebody, figuratively and literally, to say yes. Amanda remembered those meetings with a growing sense of excitement in *Vital Voices.org*. "I had a few half-baked ideas for projects centered around youth literacy and *Her Lead* believed in them before I did."

For Amanda, the *Her Lead* conference was a success and a confidence booster. "When I boarded my plane back to sunny LA, I had a new family of 49 other amazing girls, a network of phenomenal women mentors and concrete tools and skills to take back to my community."

Flying across country, Amanda was on Cloud Nine.

Chapter Six
Who is Amanda?

By the time Amanda turned 15, the dye had pretty much been cast. Her personality was set in stone.

The broad strokes. A young girl with a creative mind, quick with the word and the lines that snap, crackle and pop with emotion, a true chronicler of a period of time on the march. The countless articles about her were quick to connect the same dots. But the story, at least to that point, runs a lot deeper than that.

But even with her quickly growing fame and grand achievements at such a young age, she is still a human with her own quirks, attitudes and biases. Some of which are instinctive. Some are courtesy of her environment and her upbringing. The latter being the case when, at an early age, Amanda was beginning to look at technology as a plaything, her mother put her foot down when it came to Amanda posting excessive pictures of herself on the internet. Amanda's mother did not want her so "out there" and open to that kind of public exposure in the technological universe.

Amanda went along with her mother's wishes and, as the years have gone by, even by normal teenage standards, she has remained fairly unobtrusive as she related in a conversation with *Ten Magazine*. "I was the most reclusive teen. But it was to protect my privacy."

Amanda often reflected on her mother's agenda when it came to molding her identity and would acknowledge in *Ten Magazine* that there may well have been more of an historical leaning in how her mother raised her and her sister. "My mother gave her all to influencing the minds and hearts of a rising generation."

As the years went by, Amanda would acknowledge, that for better and worse, in addition to the challenge she faced with her speech impediment, she was also growing up as a girl inhabiting two different worlds.

"I often feel that I exist with a dichotomy inside me," she self-analyzed in *Ten Magazine*. "There is the social Amanda who is excited and talks to people and engages and then there is the poetic Amanda who, by necessity, exists off the subsistence of a reclusive life."

As she would enter her teens, it seemed that Amanda would embrace the latter as she would disclose in *Ten Magazine*. "I do not go out in general. I relax by visiting museums, watching reruns of *The Office* and *Frazier* and reading big, thick biographies. By the time everyone wants to go out, I'm already in my PJ's."

But even with an 'early to bed early to rise' ethos, Amanda could not completely avoid the trials and tribulations of her teen years as she recalled in *Trek Magazine*. "Being a teenager you're so distraught with pressures." One of the most obvious being dating and interest for the opposite sex. According to her sister Gabrielle in *Harvard Crimson*, that never seemed to be an issue for Amanda.

"It wasn't rare for men to be intimated by my sister. She was that girl that everybody knew and respected. She never tried to change herself to earn that respect. Everyone supported her for being herself."

Amanda would rarely acknowledge the more personal side of her identity and when she did, as in a story in *Harvard Crimson*, it was usually with a mixture of humor and philosophical irony.

"I proudly call myself a bitch. It's a survival mechanism."

Chapter Seven
Amanda is 16 Going on 17

By the time Amanda turned 16, there were hopes and dreams, endless possibilities to take on and to triumph over. The events of the previous year, the growth in her ability and confidence to read out loud, the publication of her first book and the overall acceptance of somebody with talent and worth was on the rise. She would give occasional guest lectures in her mother's classroom and was diligently working on her the novel. "It really opened my eyes to what I could accomplish," she told *Cultural Weekly*.

And what Amanda was continuing to feel was a kinship with the work and the spirit of Maya Angelou which had been her signpost to a bright future since the day her third grade teacher wrote a quote from Angelou on the classroom blackboard. "The quote was 'People may forget what you did but they always remember how you made them feel,'" she reflected in *Cultural Weekly*. "Whenever I feel lost in the world of writing, I try to look at the light she has shone on the job."

With her writing and the activism ingrained into her poetry now hand in hand in her life, Amanda, with seemingly a lot more on her plate then any 16-year-old, chose to expand on her good works when, with the help of *Her Lead*, she created an organization called *One Pen One Page*. Her writing program is a youth-writing and leadership program, designed to promote literacy through free creative writing pro-gramming for underserved youth. But as she would relate to *Discover Gates.org.*, activism was a big part of the *One Pen One Page* curriculum. "My goal has never been to convert every young person into a professional writer. My goal has been to make sure every young person has the literary skills they need to raise their voice and change their communities."

Amanda would be the first to admit that her sudden switch to educating was nothing new as she told *The Coven Magazine.org*. "I love to teach. My mom is a teacher so I guess I caught the bug from her. Whenever I can lead creative writing workshops, it is always a huge thrill for me."

To the point that by the time Amanda was entering her later years at *New Roads*, she was known just as much for her sense of justice and activism as she was for her writing skills. She started her own high school chapter of *Girls Learn International*, whose goal was to protect the rights of women and girls around the world. Amanda would regularly lead school assemblies and speak authoritatively on the subject of human rights abuses.

And when she felt that her 10th grade English class syllabus was lacking in what she perceived as diverse narratives, she and her sister took it upon themselves to stage a classroom revolt when they wrote a series of Disney song parodies about the lack of representation in their curriculum and presented them to their English class. Amanda recalled that moment of protest when she told the *Harvard Crimson*," I just stood up in class and said how many people feel represented in the books we are reading? Only two people raised their hands."

But at the end of the day, Amanda's writing continued to be the talk of amazement to fellow classmates and teachers alike. Gorman's 10th grade English teacher Alexandra Padilla was one of those who was constantly amazed at her young charge as she related in the *Harvard Crimson*. "I feel that by the time she came into the 10th grade she was already a writer. There was nothing I could throw at her that she couldn't tackle. She was like a firecracker."

And it would be a reputation that would spread out of the confines of Los Angeles across the country to Washington D.C., to The White House and to the attention of First Lady Michelle Obama. Obama, a long-time champion of literacy, especially among the young, launched her program *National Student Poets,* which would honor student poets from across the country with a reading at the White House hosted by the first lady. Amanda was thrilled when she received an invite in early 2016, along with four other youth poets, to come to Washington to read their poetry for an audience of dignitaries. Amanda would have a good laugh at her own expense when recalling the day with *Girl Boss.com*.

"I'm so surprised that I didn't faint. When I walked into the room and I saw her [Obama] my brain just stopped working. Someone was behind me and they were like 'Do you need to sit down?' and I was like 'I think so.' She [Obama] walked up to me and said hi and I just sputtered out 'I love you!' I was just overwhelmed. It was like standing next to a goddess."

Going into her final year at *New Roads*, there would be important decisions to be made and choices to be considered. College at a university level was a serious option and Amanda and her mother realized that higher education would be expensive. So, they set about looking into scholarship opportunities. It was in this area that Amanda proved particularly resourceful and opportunistic, as her mentor Berland would relate in *Warren-Wilson.edu.*

"Amanda was very enterprising. She picked up a flyer one day from the Milkin Family Foundation Scholarship. She found things out herself and applied. She wanted to succeed and she wanted to go to a good school."

Harvard would turn out to be that good school. It had a long-standing reputation for turning out bright, inquisitive and forward thinking minds. *Harvard* was eager to have Amanda at the university and, with the help of the Milkin Family Foundation scholarship, it sounded like Amanda was on her way to Harvard. But Amanda was not completely sold.

"I was initially unsure about attending Harvard," Amanda would remember when talking to the *Harvard Gazette*. "But then I took a trip to the campus. I saw the universities' commitment to growth and evolution and to social justice and inclusion. That visit made me think 'Maybe I can have a role in shaping these kinds of issues in our country.' I realized that Harvard was the place to be."

With her sense of activism and social justice in order, Amanda turned to that all-important issue of a major. Initially, she had thought in terms of literature and politics as a dual major. But the more daring and adventurous side of Amanda quickly took on a more important role. "The idea of majoring in literature and English seemed a bit too obvious and safe," she told the *Harvard Crimson*. "I felt like I wanted to take the risk and jump out there with something that wasn't poetry related."

And so it was that Amanda entered Harvard as a freshman late in 2016 with a major in Sociology.

Chapter Eight
New Kid on Campus

Harvard University was considered the crown jewel of the prestigious Ivy League universities. And rightfully so. Nestled in the heart of Cambridge, Massachusetts and established in 1636, Harvard University has been the starting point for a literal who's who of future presidents, statesmen and women, philosophers, giants in business and in civil rights movements, scientists and poets. Barack and Michelle Obama went to Harvard, so did John F. Kennedy, Ralph Waldo Emerson and W.E.B. DuBois are some notables. But there have been so many more whose minds and philosophies were molded in Harvard's classrooms, libraries and research centers. To be educated in Harvard was to unlock the door to a bright future.

And now it was Amanda's turn.

Entering Harvard as a freshman in 2016 was a big step. Amanda was already, by degrees, both worldly and independent. But, for the first time, she was figuratively and literally on her own. In those early days, Amanda would be cautious in trying to figure out her place in the halls of Harvard as well as where the school fit in for her. But, in short order, she would resolve that Harvard and the city of Cambridge, was the place for her. "I decided on Harvard by thinking about what mattered most to me," she offered the *Sacramento Observer*. "Harvard was a pretty diverse school for an Ivy League. Their writing department was out of this world. And I liked the idea of experiencing the East Coast."

Amanda's intellectual curiosity was immediately peaked at the prospect of entering a school where books and intellect were paramount.

"Cambridge is an oyster of intellectual and artistic thought," she offered to the *Harvard Independent*. "I am brimming with gratitude for being in that space. My world has gotten so much bigger. I look up in the sky and this openness is what it feels like to be here. It is impossible for me not to feel that the possibilities are endless."

And the notion that her chosen center for higher education was the hub of a decades-long dance with creativity and poetry was an important element of Amanda's instant love affair with the university. "It's so fantastic to be in an area with deep roots in poetry," she told the *Harvard Crimson*. "From Elizabeth Bishop to Jorie Graham to Tracy K. Smith, our country's best poets, especially women, have touched this city."

Once she was settled in, Amanda did not waste any time in establishing herself as an exacting and detail-oriented student as well as an intellectual lightning rod in the classroom. Amanda was not afraid to question what had come before and was quick to challenge the preconceived and long held Harvard's sociology curriculum. Harvard Sociology Professor Jocelyn S. Viterna recalled being particularly impressed with the way Amanda would focus on the art and passion when the topic was social reform and, over the course of time, was instrumental in expanding the way the university's sociology department thought about its approach to the subject. In an interview with *The Crimson*, Viterna also noted that Amanda, as well as other students, made significant contributions to the school's revision of the way it taught theory.

"Amanda was invested in Harvard and didn't just pass through and get her degree," she said. "Harvard was a better place because she was here and because she was thoughtful about the program and her place in the community."

Former Harvard Sociology Professor Bart Bonikowski had Amanda in his class during her freshman year and, as he would explain in an interview with *The Crimson*, he saw a lot of qualities beyond the simple fact that she was already a brilliant poet. "I saw an intellectual playfulness and a very serious goal of exposing societal flaws. She was also an exceedingly generous and kind person, a tireless activist and a topnotch researcher."

Bonikowski recalled that he had a front row seat at how passionate and driven Amanda could be during a heated discussion in his class following the election of President Donald Trump. "It was a difficult hour and I distinctly recall Amanda asking typically astute questions and also being frank about the sense of foreboding she felt about the political changes to come which would disproportionately affect communities of color."

During that first year, Amanda remained adamant about the fact that she was a sociology major even as she was peppered with questions of why, given her writing talents, she had not majored in English or something akin to poetry, effectively being at odds with the obvious assumptions about her.

"Going into college, I knew I didn't want to study English because I wanted to challenge myself to learn something new," she told *Bucknellian.net*. "Life would always pull me toward writing on its own. At Harvard, I was drawn to sociology because, as an activist, the questions that sociology asks about movement and institutions and how change operates are topics that are very central to my work."

But well into her freshman year, Amanda would find ways to balance out her school life and her writing life. Instinctively, she sought out a place of solitude where she could create in private and found her ideal local in a spot near the *Charles River*. After a long day of dealing with logic and complicated and complex theories and bouts of educational back and forth, Amanda would acknowledge in the *Harvard Advocate* that once the sun went down, she would make her way to the Charles River and meditate and create to the sound of the gently flowing waters.

"I normally write late at night, in my notebook, along the Charles River. It's often my only opportunity to just sit and be with my words and my art while the rest of the world sleeps."

Amanda's freshman year at Harvard would be an eventful one. She was thriving in her new surroundings and the outlook for her future was bright. Her growth as a poet during that first year at Harvard was also on an upward climb. The notoriety of being Los Angeles' First Youth Poet Laureate had resulted in

Amanda becoming a much in demand presence on the national spoken word scene. And with that notoriety came the first attempts at commissioned appearances from major corporations for her services.

Years later, in an extensive profile on her success with *Vogue Magazine*, Amanda would visually wince when she recalled an uncomfortable experience with the Mattel Corporation, the American multinational toy manufacturing company. The company had invited Amanda to do a public reading celebrating the arrival of their latest 'Girl of the Year' doll named Gabriela in front of a group of enthusiastic young toy buyers. Amanda, her youthful inexperience showing, readily agreed and, on the night before the reading, she received a phone call from a *Mattel* representative who briefed her on the biography of the doll.

Amanda's excitement instantly turned to horror.

The biography of Gabriela, in looks and background, was literally Amanda's life in a toy. To say that Amanda was suddenly creeped out was an understatement. A statement from Mattel's website would reinforce the fact that Gabriela was, for all intents and purposes, Amanda. "Gabriela loves the arts and uses poetry to help find her voice to make a difference in her community. Gabriela is brown skinned and has curly hair." In the *Vogue* article, an exasperated Amanda would acknowledge "She [the doll] was a Black girl with a speech impediment." Mattel in a quick strike response to Amanda's concerns stated that the Gabriela doll was not inspired by Amanda's life.

Amanda was ready to back out of the event. But, with *Vogue,* she explained why she went ahead with the reading. "I felt that if I backed out of the event, I would have been failing the girls who would have this Black doll."

But Amanda would come away from the experience more the wiser and a lesson learned about the harsh reality of popularity. "I learned that a public figure's life could be mined without her consent."

Chapter Nine
Papers Don't Write Themselves

Well into her freshman year at Harvard, Amanda had overcome her initial concerns and had quickly morphed into a confident young woman who moved easily through the maze of complexities of university life. One of the many who noticed the changes in Amanda was Laura Gorman Thomas, Harvard sociology adviser and program administrator, who in a *Harvard Crimson* article would recall the "self-assured" Amanda the first time they met. "There's something about the way she carried herself. The first thing she said to me once we introduced ourselves was 'I will be President in 2036.' And I had no doubt that she would be."

But it would not be one easy ride. Her notoriety on campus as a talented writer on the rise occasionally made her the target of what could only be petty jealousies and personal attacks from fellow students. Gorman would remember those attacks. In one poetry class, Gorman was criticized by white male classmates for being unable to understand Latin. She was particularly miffed during a seminar panel discussion when a white male classmate accused her of being too strong and too self-assured. In remembering the latter incident in the *Crimson*, Amanda would be particularly defiant.

"What frustrates me no end is that when a woman of color dares to speak up, she's framed as emotional or too domineering and I've been called that. Basically, what he was voicing was that he felt threatened by me and by my being a self-assured Black woman. And I told him that and he was like 'Well when you put it that way.' But I said 'You put it that way.'"

Amanda's approach to mixing the written and spoken word with activism and social justice had become very much a part of who she is and what drives her to make the world a better place was all about. Less than two years removed from her first published collection, *For Those Whom Food is Not Enough*, Amanda was quick to point out in a *Vice* interview that her literary and poetic world view was constantly changing. "My writing is always evolving to fit the moment, the time and the issues. I hope that 40 years from now gender disparity isn't so prevalent that I have to be writing about it. But certain values of mine will always be persistent."

And as those by now entrenched values of poetry and activism began to reach out from her regional base to a national identity, Amanda, in the best possible way, was chaffing at the possibilities. "I'm trying not to be just a teen writer, but a teen leader" she told *Ozy. com*. Not long after making that pronouncement, Amanda was offered the opportunity to exercise both sides when a creative studio called *Ozy* came calling with an offer that was right in her wheelhouse. *Ozy* had developed a reputation for looking to the future of society, both virtually and humanly and, with that, had set up the annual *Ozy Genius Award Winner* program in which 10 deserving college students are each given $10,000 grants to help them pursue their own individual ideas and dreams.

Amanda was awarded the substantial grant to develop her own creation called *Generation Empathy*, the idea of a virtual reality museum in which digital portals would allow viewers to get into the lives of young activists and how they were dealing with society's issues and challenges. Amanda's idea, born of a museum outing of her own, was simple as she would explain in *Ozy.com*. "What if there was a way in which all students, regardless of their zip code or socioeconomic status, could have field trips like that?"

And those values of inclusivity and accessibility, as well as her presence on the world stage, would certainly become enhanced in 2017 when she applied to enter the first ever competition to name the first ever National Youth Poet Laureate, a program founded in 2016 to enhance the importance of young people in shaping a future that was creatively driven in the area of poetry and spoken word as a vehicle for social justice and activism. Amanda's previous status as Los Angeles Youth Poet Laureate made her a logical choice to compete for the title. The process was an arduous one in which Amanda's written work, extracurricular activities and efforts on behalf of encouraging young people's voices in both creative and activist arenas were thoroughly vetted.

The process would reach its final step in April 2017 when Amanda and the four other finalists for the title would read at the famed Gracie Mansion in New York City. Amanda remembered that day well in a story for *Ozy.com*. "I woke up at my hotel, earlier than I liked, probably 7:00 a.m. I hadn't gotten a lot of sleep because it's finals week and that can be pretty hellish at Harvard."

After a day doing a bit of business with the *Ozy* group in the big city, Amanda made her way to Gracie Mansion where she performed her poem "Linguistics Rising" which was written after the death of Maya Angelou. This excerpt of the poem was Amanda at her most powerful, emotional and telling:

> I forgot
> All of what she said
> Yet when people asked me
> To repeat words three times
> She understood me

After what seemed like an eternity, Amanda was announced as the recipient of the title of the first National Youth Poet Laureate. Amanda was thrilled and humbled and, not surprisingly, earnest and hopeful in her acceptance speech which went worldwide in such outlets as *Poets & Writers.org*.

"For me, being able to stand on a stage as a spoken word poet, really symbolizes how, by pursuing a passion and never giving up, you can go as far as your wildest dreams. This represents such a significant moment because never, in my opinion, have the arts been more important than now."

But her selection went a lot further than a personal accomplishment as she would elaborate in a quote from *Diverseeducation.com*. "I'd been waiting for this moment to be able to connect with the youth around the country and to have a position where I could be both an activist in a community role, but also as a writer."

Following the conclusion of the ceremony, Amanda was suddenly up close and personal with the trappings of celebrity and stardom that was now hers. She would recall it in detail in *Ozy.com*.

"They announced I was National Youth Poet Laureate. And there was this craziness of being interviewed, photographed, signing things and talking to people. It was just a whirlwind of experience. I got in a taxi to go back to my hotel and I never felt such a stillness as I felt then. I almost thought that I couldn't hear anything."

The platform that would finally win the judges over was a fairly straightforward amalgamation of Amanda's approach to making the world right. It was three E's... Education, Equality and Environment, the personification of where Amanda and this time and place were heading. Amanda's voice was very much in demand and it would not take long for the celebration and the joy and the real work that went along with the title of the first National Youth Poet Laureate to begin. And for Amanda, that would mean travelling and a lot of it throughout the remainder of 2017.

"Since becoming National Youth Poet Laureate, I've been doing a lot of travelling, speaking to young people and having meetings with educators and administrators," she would recall in a *Vice* interview. "I've been doing a lot of press and a lot of interviews. I enjoy doing interviews, not necessarily for myself but because it is an opportunity for me to speak about issues that I'm passionate about."

The pace could be grueling, even for somebody of Amanda's youth and enthusiasm. In a period of nine days in September, Amanda would be a major draw in three literary and activist conferences. The Social Good Summit in which Amanda read her work "The Gathering Place," the Moth Grand Slam where she would captivate an audience with a reading of her poem "Roar" and finally what for Amanda would be a landmark reading of "In This Place: An American Lyric" as part of a Library of Congress ceremony honoring the achievements of one of her idols, poet Tracy K. Smith.

Amanda recalled in a *Library of Congress.gov* newsletter blog that the significance of that reading put her title and attitude towards it in a joking deprecating state of mind. "National Youth Poet Laureate is a title too long to mention casually at dinner parties. It was other worldly to be the first US Youth Poet Laureate to be invited to speak at a place like the Library of Congress. Since I'm the first one, people don't often know the US Youth Poet Laureate exists. It's kind of like being a unicorn."

The actual reading of her poem went by in a blur. She admitted in her *Library of Congress blog* that she did not remember much of her performance other than the standing ovation she received at its conclusion. "But getting a standing ovation at the Library of Congress was pretty spectacular. It was one of the moments I slip into my pocket for when I'm stressed out about a Government [class] exam."

That quote above was just a reminder that Amanda, now the darling of the literary world, was in fact carrying a full load of challenging classes going into her second year at Harvard. It would be the yin and yang of her now very full life that she would address in a *Brit&Co. com* interview. "Being a full-time student at Harvard, [but] I'll be travelling to places like Colorado, California and New York City. But, at the same-time, I also have a paper that's due that's not going to write itself. I'm in love with poetry and sharing it with others. But I'm also someone who is in love with learning and being a student."

Chapter Ten
Have Poems Will Travel

By the time Amanda turned 19, she had, for all intents and purposes, arrived as a young woman of substance, talent and no small amount of influence on the changing times. This was much in evidence with her coronation as the first US National Youth Poet Laureate. But as Amanda would acknowledge when talking to *The Root.com*, the title was a double-edged sword. "It [the title] was a lot of pressure. But, at the same time, it was a huge platform I felt I could use to make changes."

And with the title, there would be concern among many observers that the inherent accolades coupled with a very impressionable young mind could blunt Amanda's pure creative instincts. But as Amanda would explain to *Yahoo.com*, there was nothing to fear on that account. "I think for me personally, accomplishment exists in a wider pursuit that I'm most proud of, which is continuing in the tradition of storytelling outlined by my ancestors and not letting race, gender, class or small-minded prejudice stop me."

With that attitude firmly in place, Amanda set out into a world that had discovered her and was now demanding all she could give. Which suddenly made her the go to poet when it came to paying for commissioned poetry, a potentially slippery slope that to many would smack of commercial influence and, worst of all, compromise of what has always been considered a monastic, serious, above it all occupation. But Amanda would insist that poetry for pay was a legitimate venture to her way of thinking and, when created in a climate that was her own, was every bit as challenging as her more austere work.

"There's a period of intense study and research," she offered *The Harvard Gazette*, "followed by a period of seclusion. Then I begin to shape." And she was quite capable of putting a logical spin on her commissioned work when she continued in *The Harvard Gazette* "My job is to coax people into my lyricism without them realizing they are listening to a poem I hope that happens."

Two thousand eighteen would be a determining period in which Amanda would find herself immersed in non-stop appearances and readings, both commercial and pure. And if early appearances were any indication, Amanda came fully prepared to do the right thing.

Especially when it came close to home. Lawrence S. Bacow had just been named Harvard University President and Amanda was asked to create a poem to be read at his inauguration ceremony. Amanda dug deep into the tradition of the university and, perhaps more importantly, what Harvard meant to those that passed through its hallowed halls. An excerpt from the completed poem that appeared in *CulturedMagazine.org* made that point.

When the mind is free
When we take another look
We see that the books are open
The silence of a blank page broken
By truth being shared, written, spoken

An early commission was to be written and performed at the Revlon Live Boldly Campaign launch. Amanda reasoned that what appeared to be a thinly veiled marketing campaign did have, at its core, an important statement to be made about women coming of age and would say as much, as witness this excerpt from the poem she read.

When I see young women I see their glow
From their impact
How they act
What they do
And what they know

Throughout the spring and summer, Amanda was in a literal whirlwind of duties and opportunities created, in large part, by her position as the first US Youth National Poet Laureate. At the request of the famed Morgan Library and Museum, she went to the New York library in March, with handwritten notes tied to the poem "In This Place (An American Lyric)" in tow to donate them to an ongoing exhibit of rarities tied to the work of famous women writers and poets.

She then would have an emotional return to Los Angeles in April where she would read a poem by one of the victims of the mass shooting at Marjory Stoneman Douglas High School. The summer would remain a busy time where she would balance commissioned work with socially activist related appearances and the ever-present specter of a being a sociology major at Harvard with a 4.0 GPA to keep up.

Amanda took part in a reading of letters by the late South African President Nelson Mandela, represent during the BET Black Girls Rock awards show and, on the commissioned work side, would read her pro-climate change poem Earthrise in front of former Vice President and progressive climate advocate Al Gore during the Climate Reality Project confab. Amanda would also wax nostalgic and sentimental with her poem "The Playhouse" during a ceremony honoring legendary actor Dick Van Dyke and Broadway superstar Lin Manuel Miranda.

In a classic bit of understatement, Amanda would acknowledge her workload in conversation with *LA Taco.com* when she said, "I guess I have a lot going on."

Her presence out front and very much in an activist vein would continue, performing at the Conference of World Affairs at the University of Colorado and the March On Washington Film Festival while literally hopscotching across the United States to read at a number of events, both big and small.

Amanda was well aware that she was getting the kind of attention and opportunities normally reserved for rock stars and movie and television celebrities. On one level she was in awe of it all, the young girl enthralled and thrilled at what was being presented in front of her. But there was also a more enlightened thoughtful side to Amanda as she soaked up the adulation and attention in conversation with *The Crimson*.

"I'm standing on the shoulders of people who

broke their backs to get me here, so that I could see further. God forbid that I throw this shot away."

Chapter Eleven
Amanda Finds Herself

Going into 2019, Amanda was looking for something different, something to challenge her and her feelings about herself and her place in the world. Literally broadening her horizons seemed a logical next step. Which was why, in the midst of everything that being Amanda Gorman had become on a national and international stage, she decided to take a semester away from the Harvard campus and go to Spain to study. Amanda would couch her experience in Madrid, describing her trip as much of a spiritual journey as it was an educational one in *IES Abroad.org*.

"My passion for coming to Spain was so much larger than just being in a classroom. It was about how this experience would make me a better poet, a better person and a better student. It was so life changing and phenomenal, I don't think I would be who I am today without that experience."

Amanda's time abroad would be a time of reflection and looking inward as the young girl examined who she was, what she had become and, most importantly, what she could do to improve herself. And, as she explained in *The Observer*, she came to a hard truth about herself. "When I think about what I'm most afraid to write about, it's about me and my life. For a long time, I've put up a wall around that so now I'm trying to dig into that."

It would not be all work and no play during her time in Madrid. Her connections as National Youth Poet Laureate had led her to contacts in the fashion world and, in February 2019, she received an invitation from top fashion designer Prada to travel to Milan, Italy to take in the sights and sounds of Milan Fashion Week. Amanda was a bit taken aback by the invitation. "Poets aren't well represented in the fashion world," she told *Vogue*, "let alone young female poets of color. There's this idea of the poor, suffering poet and I try to exhibit that the poet can be stylish too. When I'm performing onstage, I'm not just thinking about my clothing but what my clothing is saying about my identity as a poet."

As it turned out, Amanda was able to combine fashion and poetry during her Milan vacation when she wrote "A Poet's Prada" which appeared in *Vogue* and, as this excerpt shows, was a deft chronicle of what she experienced.

> Seeking: Well-crafted, high-end
> Fashion that transcends trends
>
> Looking: To challenge fashion codes
> Dance off previously carved roads
> Unafraid to experiment, explore, explode

Amanda would return to the states after her time abroad seemingly invigorated at the prospect of who she was and what she could do with her poetry and her life. Not that she had ever been anything less than enthusiastic about any of the opportunities that had come her way. But now, both emotionally and spiritually, there seemed to be that little extra spring in her step and a wider ranging and all-encompassing outlook on what was to come.

"I've always hoped that through my tenure [as US National Youth Poet Laureate] that I've been able to bring youthful poetry into new and unexpected places," she would state in *Assembly.Malala.org*. And in 2019, it appeared that she was doing just that.

The media not only began looking to her as a pop culture icon to be poked and prodded but also as a literary light of some legitimacy who had a mind worth cultivating. *The New York Times* would come calling with the enticing offer of having Amanda write opinion columns for their newsletter called *The Edit.* Poetry and activism would go hand in hand throughout the never-ending series of appearances and readings throughout the rest of the year.

And even as her notoriety as a poet for the ages grew, Amanda would often chaff at the notion that, in the eyes of many, she was a poet and she would often hint that there was more going on in her psyche then the written word on a page. "My family already knows that I'm interdisciplinary," she quipped to *The Observer*. "But I don't think the world knows it yet. There's a lot of things that make up the shape of who we are. I'm just trying to invite them in and write them down."

She would stake her claim for creative independence on April 10, 2019 during a reading at the Women in the World Summit when she gave a multidimensional reading that incorporated spoken word, music and a deft bit of dance/choreography courtesy of award winning dance choreographer, Sherrie Silver.

July 4th would see Amanda continuing to stretch the boundaries of spoken word when she read a rousing version of "Hymn for The Republic" backed by the Boston Pops Orchestra. And in a subtle but no less inspiring reading in tribute to the Empire State Building, Amanda, backed by the tasteful piano passages of musician Jon Batiste, made a powerful statement with her poem "The Republic Rising."

This series of multimedia readings caught the attention of observers and would be the topic of much conversation and debate in the ensuing months. Was Amanda venturing too far into the realm of pop sensibilities at the expense of the power of the word? Amanda, in conversation with *The Observer*, did not think so. In fact, she believed these flights of poetic fancy were part of her master plan. "I'm always trying to remind people that I'm so much more than just a poet. I haven't even been a poet a long time in this short life that I've lived."

But the fact that she was becoming a well-known personality in the mainstream world, far away from the stereotypical isolated, ivory tower image of a poet, Amanda was not about to let her strong activism take a backseat. As part of one of her steps into the business world, Amanda would appear at the Prada Shaping the Future conference. This was a very business-oriented agenda combined with how commercial interests could be used for the betterment of society. Nevertheless, at the conference to report on a fact finding trip to Slovenia, Amanda did step forward to speak her mind on the deeper societal issues of what this conference should represent.

"Freedom is not necessarily just the economic freedom of what I'm going to purchase. When young people talk about the liberation of the world, it's not just I want freedom for myself. It's I want freedom for my neighbor. I want freedom for people who look different from me or who speak a different culture."

Amanda would be in full feminist form when she read her poem "The Way Forward" during the mid-year *Forbes Magazine* Women's Summit to an appreciative audience of women from the business and activist world. Typical of her ever-evolving reading style, Amanda was straightforward, emotional and varying degrees of challenging and defiant as she read the following excerpt from "The Way Forward."

> Forged forth by a future that is female.
>
> We will not be slowed, come the loads, the roadblocks that may.
>
> We'll keep fulfilling this path
>
> Until the world goes still to say:
>
> Where there's will, there's women
>
> And where there's woman
>
> There is always a way.

There was an inevitability to Amanda's life at that point. The power of her words could not be denied. The awards and year-end lists were beginning to swirl around the young girl. The influential *Roots Magazine* was a significant example, naming Amanda to their Young Futurists list, an annual proclamation of the top 25 African Americans who were exceling in the fields of social justice and activism.

It would be attention on a worldwide level that,

not surprisingly, brought the first ripples of interest from major book publishers that were growing more competitive by the moment. According to reports of the time, as many as eight major publishers were reportedly throwing around monetary figures that were light years removed from the normal poet/publisher transactions. In June 2019, it would be announced that Amanda had signed a two-book deal with Viking Books for publication set for 2021.

Amanda was aware of what was going on. But she was, by the end of 2019, back at Harvard, grinding it out as a third-year sociology major and, as much as possible, trying to balance out her everyday reality with her growing notoriety and, lest it be said, celebrity and stardom. Whatever Amanda was dealing with at the moment was serious business that required her undivided attention. She would insist to anybody who asked that whatever was going on in her life, it was all about the writing, cultivating some ideas for books and hoping to get her ducks in order before her senior year at Harvard came around and her final papers were due.

It was all that had been 2019 that Amanda would, jokingly, put in perspective when she talked to *Cultured Magazine*.

"I need an auto response on my email that says 'I'm studying. I'm in school. Catch up with you later.'"

Chapter Twelve
2020 Over and Out

It was nearing the end of 2020 and Amanda had no idea what to do.

Harper's Bazaar magazine had commissioned Amanda to do an opinion piece, reflecting on the year that would soon end. And as she would candidly reveal when she did finally put pen to paper, "I had no idea what to write." Which, in a sense, was surprising. 2020 had been ripe with things to chronicle and be opinionated about. There were social and political tensions galore. Police were killing Black people with upsetting regularity. Black Lives Matter was a viable and often maligned group both on the rise and on the march. And it goes without saying that the Corona virus pandemic that was laying waste to the world had a definite impact on everyday lives. The country and the world for that matter had become tribal with everybody taking up sides and casting aspersions on the other. The list of things to discourse on was seemingly endless and everywhere.

But Amanda was having a hard time wrapping her mind and thoughts around it. And so, for a time, she did what we've all done at one point or another in our lives. She procrastinated. Amanda would concede that, for a time, she binge-watched a lot of television, did a lot of laundry and walked her dog a lot. And while she was finally able to write a piece that effectively explored the personal and poetic meaning of what 2020 had been, internally Amanda was still struggling with her place in a year that had, to a large extent, spiraled out of control.

"It was March 11, a day that will live in infamy." Amanda related in *Diverseeducation.com*. It was the day that the Corona virus had reached pandemic levels. It was the day that Harvard shuttered its doors and the students were sent away. Amanda would return to Los Angeles and would, subsequently, shelter in place with her mother and sister.

She would spend her days in isolation, writing, planting a small indoor garden and studying for her final exams. But she soon realized that her life, as well as countless others, were now wrapped around an encroaching pandemic that was wrecking havoc on those who were being brought to an emotional edge of being on lockdown—out of work, possible eviction and the newness of standing in line for hours to get food as the sickness and death tolls mounted. It was all too much and it was crying out for a statement.

Over a period of three days in April, Amanda crafted the poem "The Miracle of Morning," a statement very much in Amanda's realm of thinking and believing, dealing with the often harsh reality while pointing toward the power to heal and change for the better around the notions of peace, love and hope. Like all of Amanda's more significant writings, "The Miracle of Morning" would be an arduous challenge that required an extensive amount of research that included looking to

Martin Luther King's "I Have A Dream" speech, Maya Angelou's "On the Pulse of Morning" poem and the sonnets of Shakespeare for inspiration as she explained in *Diverseeducation.com*.

"As I was writing the poem and trying to think of images, words and language, I was also trying to think of a visual and linguistic rhetoric that all spoke to the idea of love. It really just came out organically out of the things that I was seeing and recognizing as positive, worthwhile and inspiring during this time. While I was writing, I would look out onto the street and really try to internalize what I was viewing and what was going on out there."

Creating "The Miracle of Morning" would be a Herculean emotional task for Amanda which, as she explained to *Diverseeducation.com*, literally drove her into isolation. "I wrote the poem when I was in the park, deciding to spend my outdoor time separate and alone, watching other people. I was suffused with this imagery of separate but close."

And as she would relate in a *WGBH News.com* conversation, the genesis of the poem was very much immersed in history and her Black heritage. "I was thinking about Martin Luther King, writing from a Birmingham jail on racial injustice. I was thinking about Nelson Mandela writing and reading while he was in jail for decades. I was thinking about Anne Frank writing as she was hiding from Nazis. I was thinking about what humans do when they are scared, alone and isolated from the rest of the world."

Amanda would unveil "The Miracle of Morning" in April with a public reading at the Los Angeles Central Library. And the result, as depicted in this excerpt by *PBS*, was a taut, fiery exercise full of hope and the power to survive and prosper.

> While we might feel small, separate and all alone,
>
> Our people have never been more closely tethered.
>
> The question isn't whether we can weather this unknown,
>
> But how we will weather this unknown together.
>
> So on this meaningful morn, we mourn and we mend.

"2020! What a year!" Amanda would reveal in *Harpers Bazar*. "It was rough on all of us but as a public poet, people don't see the reality of my life. They see, maybe, a poem or a recital and it's great to hear that I can serve as a ray of light. But sometimes it grabs attention away from the fact that [through 2020] I was going through some of the same things and the darkness as well. It was really a hard time when my school was shut down in March when the Corona wave crested. I wasn't going to have a normal graduation and I wasn't going to be able to say goodbye to my friends."

But ever the optimist, Amanda was ultimately able to look past the negativity to something new that was emerging in the way she approached life and the written world as she explored in her *Harpers Bazaar* reflection. "The climate, not only the pandemic, but also the racial and political tension have added a new layer of responsibility in my own work. Now I have to interweave my poetry with a sense of purpose."

And it would be that coming of age attitude that would see Amanda flower during what was her senior year at Harvard that forced her to continue amid the pandemic as she normally had. There continued to be her duties as Poet Laureate that would regularly take her away from campus but, as she offered to *The Project for Women.com* "I'm trying to keep myself grounded at school. I don't want to slack off on my studies."

And Amanda would be as good as her word.

Her final year at Harvard, up until the pandemic forced the world to act differently, would be a time of deep dedication and self-evaluation in which Amanda reaffirmed her notion that the concepts of poetry and the hard and fast ideas of sociology would go hand in hand.

Jocelyn Viterna, Amanda's former sociology teacher, would acknowledge her student's dedication to combining the forms in conversation with *American Sociological Association.org.* "Amanda often talks about doing her research before she writes a poem and I'd like to think that her commitment is what drew her to sociology. Throughout college, Amanda sought to ground her art in the sociological understanding of research design, politics, activism, poverty and racial inequalities."

Amanda graduated with honors at Harvard University in May 2020. There would be no grand ceremony with friends and teachers congratulating each other and wishing each other well amid the pomp and circumstance of graduations gone by. Amanda's final memory of Harvard would be played out in a virtual ceremony and the last images she would have would be by way of Zoom. Amanda was, like her poetry, looking from both sides at the irony that had resulted in a virtual graduation, one that cost her the opportunity to be with her friends and classmates one last time. But she would also be hopeful in the bright future she saw for herself.

"Ceremony or not, I'm looking forward to getting my diploma and degree," she offered *Diverse education.com* shortly before graduating. "I've worked hard for it and my family has invested so much time, energy and money into it. I'm really looking forward to saying I did this."

And she knew that leaving Harvard would be a mighty step toward independence. She was now officially on her own in the world, not tied in any way to the life of a student. Amanda now truly had to make her life as a full-time writer. And she would not have to wait long to see that dream become a reality.

Midway through June, it would be announced that Amanda had closed a two-book publishing deal with Viking Books with a publication date of 2021. While no information regarding the dollars and cents of the deal was forthcoming, it was safe to say that Amanda was now a professional author. And as it turned out, the first of the two books was already completed. Long before the onset of the pandemic.

Amanda had conceived of an idea for a children's picture book called *Changes Sing: A Child's Anthem*, a picture book that mixes text and illustrations to tell the story of a young girl who leads a cast of characters on a musical journey as they learn they have the power to make changes in the world.

"It's a children's anthem but I'm speaking to the times we live in," Amanda explained to *Diverse education.com*. "I felt the children of this generation deserved something that spoke to them."

Amanda would spend the remaining months of 2020 in a state of creative bliss. With a book deal and a sudden influx of advisers that she would often refer to as "her team" (agents, publicists, and all manner of people to both guide her and shield her from the pressures of being in the spotlight) in her creative back pocket, Amanda was free to be and do whatever she wanted.

She had become more media savvy in the ensuing months and her youth and natural enthusiasm for what she was about and what her role in the world was that she quickly became in demand by the mainstream media and television talk shows. Amanda was a quick study on the latter, offering up the expected backstory answers in a way that gave the impression that she was hearing the question for the first time. There would be the moments when she was being offered the spotlight to read her poetry and the likes of "Rise" and "Fury and Faith," recited with sincerity and believability amid the hot television studio lights were a gateway to that larger world where poetry had always been an afterthought or an alien life form but, with her elevation to celebrity status in a pop culture world, was suddenly something people were seeking out as insightful and important light years removed from the notion of hip.

In a way, Amanda was suddenly feeling the power, in the best possible way, that her words and her presence could bring. Amanda was suddenly feeling important and, perhaps, a bit full of herself. So much so that when the Bidens called with the invitation to perform at the presidential inaugural ceremonies, no one was too surprised when Amanda told *Vogue* after accepting the invitation that…

"I'm not saying I'm better than anybody else but I was called by the Bidens for a reason. This moment has called me for a reason. All I can do is show up and do my absolute best. That's all I can ask of myself."

Chapter Thirteen
Six Minutes and Counting

It was not long after receiving the invitation of a lifetime that reality set in for Amanda.

She was about to become a moment in history that would forever be part of the ages. Now all she had to do was write like she had never written before. And those early days were slow going as she recalled in an interview with National Public Radio, days of referencing historical influences and looking for the psycho-logical and emotional hook that had served her well in the past.

"It was really daunting to begin the poem," recalled Amanda, "because I didn't even know the entry point in which to step into the murk."

But Amanda had been down this road before.

Research had always been a challenge, the inevitable tussle that was the lynchpin that she had to conquer before the first word was written. And so, her confidence in her ability to write the poem grew as, day by day, she chipped away as the concept for the poem came together and began to make sense. But as she recalled during an interview with *BBC Breakfast* [TV], the struggle was far from over.

"I had no idea what the poem was called. I was just writing it in My Documents folder and it was like 'The

Inaugural Poem,' you know very descriptive. I didn't
know what the title was and it wasn't until I had finished
the poem, that I looked at the line that said 'The hill we
climb only if we dare' and I was like 'that's it.'"

Well into 2021, Amanda was a creative dervish.

The poem was now complete. It had a title and,
with the events of January 6 driving it home, Amanda
only had one more obstacle to overcome as she related
to *BBC Breakfast*. "When I began writing 'The Hill
We Climb,' I had only five minutes of allotted time.
But after January 6, I was like 'This poem is six minutes and it's going to stay that way because there's
actually a lot more that needs to be said.'" She would
further put her creative foot down on the matter of
time when she stood tall in telling National Public
Radio. "After January 6, I was like 'Well this is something we need to talk about.'"

In her own mind, Amanda, with the completion
of "The Hill We Climb," had seemingly arrived at the
crossroads of talent and purpose. Her words and the
poem were all powerful. The message and the defiant
yet hopeful tone of her activism was upfront for all to
experience and process. Amanda was very much in the
moment when she told *The Washington Post*, "My
hope is that my poem will represent a moment of unity
for our country."

And as her mother and Amanda boarded the plane
that would take them to Washington D.C., Amanda,
after mentally rehearsing her reading for the umpteenth
time, was confident that she had gotten it right. "I'm not
going to gloss over what we've seen in the past few
weeks," she told the *New York Times* just days before
the inauguration. "What I really aspire to in the poem is

to be able to use my words to envision a way in which our country can come together and heal."

The day of the inauguration, Amanda was admittedly star-struck as she prepared for her moment. She was rubbing shoulders with Barack and Michelle Obama, Lady Gaga, and all manner of politicians and Washington's elite and influential in the world of politics, societal and social importance. But all that was put aside when it was time to step to the podium to read "The Hill We Climb." Amanda was trans-formed into a young woman of purpose and promise, offering her words in a world that sorely needed both. As she spoke the first words of "The Hill We Climb," she was all business.

Over the next six minutes, Amanda's life would change forever. When she began reading, Amanda had been a somewhat known poet, still known primarily through literary and academic circles, who was just beginning to make inroads into the mainstream. At one point during her reading of "The Hill We Climb," the world of social media suddenly erupted, catapulting Amanda to the level of national obsession in a matter of minutes. Shortly after completing her reading to resounding applause and congratulations from some of the most well-known people on the planet, Amanda and her mother would be ushered away from the ceremony and into a private room where, upon checking her Instagram and Twitter accounts, Amanda would discover the degree in which she had suddenly been discovered by the world.

She had jumped from 100,000 Twitter followers to 1.2 million and from 206,000 Instagram followers to 2.4 million. The internet acceptance was palpable, and Amanda would concede in subsequent interviews with *S Magazine* and *CNN*, she attempted to make sense of it all, internally and externally. "I learned [at that moment] about the power of language to start social movements, energize revolutions and bring about widespread change. I came here [to the inauguration] to do the best with the poem that I could. And to see the support that's been pouring out, I literally can't absorb it all. So I'll be processing it all for a while."

Amanda would do a whole lot of processing on her flight home the next day. Her Twitter account remained on fire. She was getting excited messages from people she knew and did not know. There were the expected congratulatory missives and what would be the first rush of interview requests from the top tier television shows. Even before her plane touched down in Los Angeles, Amanda was already feeling the rush of instant celebrity when it was announced that her two books, *Changes Sing: A Child's Anthem* (which was not yet completed) and *The Hill We Climb and Other Poems* (which, except for the title poem, was not yet completely written) had immediately emerged on the Amazon Preorder rankings as No. One and No. Two respectfully, months ahead of their actual publication date.

Amanda would later tweet about how the Amazon announcement had, joyously, knocked her for a loop. "I was on the floor. My books are number one and number two on Amazon after one day. All I can say is thank you for supporting me and my words."

Amanda descended the gangway at Los Angeles International Airport and was greeted by her sister Gabrielle who was singing and holding their dog up in the air much like the scene in *The Lion King*. It was a sign that things were about to change but it was also a sign that all the fame and celebrity that would most certainly follow would never replace that feeling of being back in the real world with her family that, in every possible way, stood in support for her.

"My mom and my sister, they're always my rock," she told *BBC Breakfast*. "And then there's my dog, Lulu. Because of her nothing's changed. I still have to pick up her poop."

The next week would be a blur of happy talk on the talk show circuit where the biggest names in the media would ask Amanda to relive the moment and, by association, the events in her life that had led her to the inauguration. In lesser hands, this whirlwind of promotion and celebration might have been too much to handle for the young woman suddenly thrust into history. But by this time, Amanda was an old hand at the interview process and the constant challenge of dealing with essentially the same questions over and over. Point of fact, Amanda seemed anxious to get in front of the press and was quick to use every opportunity to advance her attitudes toward social justice and her own brand of activism. Inevitably, there would be the softball questions, the obvious questions of just how it all felt to be a part of a historical moment. And, in those moments, Amanda shed all pretense of the seriousness of the moment and was once again the enthusiastic and sincere young girl.

"What a day! What a life! Thank you! Thank you!" she excitedly told the *New York Post*. Amanda would be equally effusive on the television talk show *Good Morning America*. "It's not often that you wake up on a morning feeling like this. I had never been expecting that at 22, that they would trust me with such an honor."

It was like the world had caught lighting in the bottle. Viking, already sensing a firestorm of interest, had quickly commissioned a stand-alone special edition of the poem "The Hill We Climb," complete with a forward by Amanda's unofficial mentor and guiding light Oprah Winfrey, to be released April 27. But within a week of the inauguration, the release of the book was moved up to March 16.

Some weeks before the release of that book, Amanda had already taken the next big step as the pop culture poet when, on February 7, she read an original poem entitled "Chorus of the Captains" prior to the Super Bowl as part of a pre-game ceremony honoring three essential workers—an educator, a marine veteran and a nurse—as the NFL honored the true heroes of the COVID pandemic. The poem was heartfelt and reflected hope as it thanked those in the frontlines and in the trenches. And emblematic of Amanda and her rise to the status of literary and pop culture icon, Amanda's reading of "Chorus of the Captains" was reportedly witnessed by more than 100 million viewers around the world. As always, there would be some traditionalists who looked askance at the idea of a poet reading serious work before a professional football game.

But in a Tweet shortly after the event, Amanda would make a spirited defense about how tying football and poetry together all made sense. "Poetry at the Super Bowl is a feat for art and our country. It means we're thinking imaginatively about human connection, even when we feel siloed. I honor three heroes who exemplify the best of this effort."

Late in February, a bit of a controversy emerged surrounding the translation of "The Hill We Climb" into foreign languages emerged that would bring Amanda back to the business side of her art. As reported in *BBC News* and *The Guardian*, Dutch writer Marieke Lucas Rijnevgeld, who had reportedly been approved by Amanda to do the Dutch translation of "The Hill We Climb," unexpectedly stepped down from the assignment amid a wave of media criticism about the ethics and, yes, politics of a white male writer translating the work of a Black, female writer. In March 2021, the controversy continued when, after completing the Catalan language translation for a Spanish publisher of "The Hill We Climb," writer Victor Obilos was, unexpectedly, removed from the project, reportedly on orders from Amanda's US publisher *Viking*, on the grounds that Obilos' effort was marred by the fact that he, like Rijnevgeld, was a white male. Many observers of the situation questioned the sense of reverse discrimination, but the controversy would quickly die on its own accord.

Amanda would continue to navigate the non-traditional opportunities not normally afforded women of letters when she signed with the star making *IMG Modeling* agency, the place where fashion is king and their clients are some of the most well-known women in the world. On the surface, it appeared to be a well-intentioned but economically driven move in which Amanda would work with the agency on a variety of fashion-related endorsements and ad campaigns. But in a conversation with *Vogue*, Amanda would insist that there was a correlation between poetry and fashion that fit her way of viewing the world around her.

"Fashion has so much meaning for me and it's my way to lean into the history that came before me and all the people supporting me."

Amanda was in the middle of a whirlwind of interest and offers. There was the much-trumpeted cover story for *Time Magazine* in which she was interviewed by Michelle Obama in which the expected hoopla was replaced by an insightful discourse focusing on activism and social justice. She would sit down with Oprah Winfrey for a far-reaching interview that also dug deep into her psyche. By the end of May, she had already committed to an appearance at the Professional Business Women of California Conference and was recently announced as one of a handful of suddenly youthful co-hosts to host the Met Gala in September. There had even been an offer from a university of a full-time teaching residence position from Morgan State University that, in hindsight, seemed more a shot in the dark by the university than anything approaching a legitimate offer.

Amanda, in a statement tinged with understatement, acknowledged in a *Vogue* interview that people and offers were everywhere she turned. "I think I'm going to be on a rollercoaster for a while. But I'm looking forward to absorbing everything that will happen. I'm definitely journaling about it, writing more poetry about it. I'll be coming out with a poetry collection later this year so a lot of that [what she's experiencing] will be processed in that work."

Chapter Fourteen
Hiding Out

Oprah Winfrey had become a very important and, yes, influential person in Amanda's life at a time when it seemed that everybody and their mother was attempting just that in the post inauguration rush to get to Amanda, the perceived next big thing. Oprah had been a gentle, yet persuasive voice in Amanda's ear well before the inauguration and, to the young woman's way of thinking, had presented herself as a humane mentor. That common sense and a sense of down-home objectivity, was seemingly just what Amanda needed at a time when things were starting to get a bit hectic in Amanda's life.

And Amanda was receptive to everything Oprah had to say. During an extensive interview with Oprah for her television series *The Oprah Conversations*, the veteran talk show moderator offered Amanda a particularly pointed bit of advice which Amanda would recall during an extensive interview with *Vogue*. "Oprah gave me a great piece of advice when she told me to be weary of other people's agendas because they all have them."

And as things ramped up in her life during 2021, Amanda's mantra when it came to making decisions would be 'What would Oprah do?' There would be many occasions when Amanda would intone that phrase. As with any new cultural phenomena, Amanda was being flooded with financial opportunities to consider, a normal situation in the pop culture world in which 'the next big thing' is tempted to strike while the iron is hot. But Amanda was cut from different cloth than the normally mercenary instincts of rock stars and actors. She was an author and like most authors, was in her career for the long haul. And so, her attitude toward making money off her creativity was a lot more pragmatic.

Already a seasoned pro when it came to taking on commissioned work, Amanda was now being particular at what she chose to take on, explaining matter of factly to *Vogue* that she had already turned down more than $17 million in endorsement deals and, with the aid of her advisors, was taking great pains to only do things that made sense to her social justice and activist sensibilities.

"I didn't really look at the details [of the offers] because if you see something and it says a million dollars, you're going to rationalize why that makes sense," she told *Vogue*. "I have to be conscious of taking commissions that speak to me."

And as recent events were playing out, Amanda could afford to be choosey. By May 2021, the stand-alone edition of "The Hill We Climb" had already spent nearly four weeks at or near the top of the *New York Times* Bestseller List and was giving every indication that it would be around for a while.

Through much of the year, Amanda would do her best to both deal with and cope. When not on the road for a professional commission or engagement, she would inevitably find her way back to Los Angeles and the comfort and support of her family. She had her favorite trails to walk that usually brought her in contact with the Pacific Ocean and a few moments of contemplation. She was occasionally spotted in her travels around town, but the hysteria had seemed to have plateaued. When she is recognized in her neighborhood now, it's usually in a respectful manner. But she is never usually far or very long from a phone call from her advisors, with the news of a possible commission or an interview request.

Not surprisingly, there has been the often idol speculation about what was next, opinion pieces that are usually intended to pontificate on a career that has been decades in the making rather than the meteoric rise of somebody who has just turned 23. There have been some shots taken, not too veiled diatribes about the marketing of yet another pop culture celebrity. In her more introspective moments, Amanda takes it all in, the good and the not so good. Admittedly, she knows that there is a bright future on the horizon and the possibilities are endless. But there are those moments when all Amanda can muster is what she would tell *Vogue* in a clipped response to dealing with pressure and contradictions in her life.

"It's complicated."

Chapter Fifteen
No is a Complete Sentence

"It's complicated."

Yes, the answer was vague. More of a mystery or a deliberate sidestep than a definitive response. Maybe, for those inclined to read between the lines, an attempt to deflect from a response that might hit on something Amanda was not comfortable with.

But the reality remained more than the notion of evasiveness going into 2021. Not only was Amanda comfortable with her life and her world and not losing sleep over any of it. She was at peace. A true sign of contentment would be that, to those who were around her or talked to her, Amanda was handling stardom and worldwide adulation quite well and had grown into quite the literary professional in the process. Exhibit A?

Amanda had survived a nearly a year-long media tidal wave with nary a hiccup or stumble and was quick to discover how to play the game like a seasoned pro.

Her two books, slated for a September 2021 release, are in the final stage of preparation. Interest in her remained high but, by mid-May, had dissolved to a manageable level. By degrees, she was now out and about in her life, never completely free of the recognition as somebody special but free enough in her own mind to take moments to sit back and reflect on the notion that she has become a beacon for the future on poetic and activist fronts.

Amanda has often conceded that her success to this point has been a lot of hard work and perseverance. It's moments like these that Amanda is to the point. There is no ego in her words. No brag involved. It's just facts and a lot of words and she is very Amanda-like in those moments in acknowledging that she could not have gotten this far on her own.

"It took a lot of work," she modestly told *Vogue*. "Not only on my part but also on my family and my village to get here."

And one of the first things Amanda would admit to is that to get here, with all the accolades currently coming her way, she still does not completely get it as she explained, with more of a philosophical take, in the recent *Time* magazine interview. "I'm new to this and I'm still learning. I would say that anyone who finds themselves suddenly visible and suddenly famous should look at the big picture. I have to crown myself with the belief that what I'm about and what I'm here for is way beyond this moment."

She does concede that her position of influence in a world looking for guidance can be a bit overwhelming at times. People have questions. People want to know what to do. People want the word from on high as they figure only Amanda can deliver it. In other words...

For better or worse, Amanda acknowledged that she has become a role model and, not surprisingly, it is a crown that does not always sit easily on her head. She recalled as far back as 2017 in conversation with *The Sacramento Observer* that in her early days as US National Youth Poet Laureate she was already being considered a role model in many circles and that she did feel a degree of pressure and responsibility that carries over to this day.

"Usually after one of my talks or readings, the students come up and thank me. I feel like I should be thanking them. It's the soul, strength and spirit of girls of color. I walk out of a room of confident young Black girls and feel rejuvenated and ready to take on the world with them. I take the idea of being a role model very seriously. It's my responsibility to radiate some light in the darkness."

Those expectations have followed Amanda into the later years and the ebbs and flows of social justice and activism on the march in the United States and around the world. To her way of thinking, the Biden Inauguration was only the pinnacle of a long arduous real-world struggle. These days, Amanda prides herself as being part of a social and historical continuum that has flowered in 2021 but, as she offered in the *Time* magazine interview with Michelle Obama, makes her part of a natural evolution.

"What's been exciting for me is that I get to absorb and to live in the creation I see from other African American artists who I look up to. But then I also get to create art and to participate in that historical record. I can't imagine anything more exciting than that."

Amanda seemed always at ease when discussing the more deep, insightful aspects of what she does than the questions of a softer, pop culture nature that, in recent months, she's come to be used to. But she had often slipped into a more thoughtful, more personal sense of being when discussing what she does on a more intellectual level.

"I really want to use my words to be a point of unity, collaboration and togetherness," she would insist in a conversation with *BBC.com*. "I think it's about a new chapter, about the future and doing that through the elegance and beauty of words."

And it does not come as much of a surprise when a spirit of religious fervor often slips into her deeper thoughts. One such conversation with *Vatican News.com* would bring the enlightenment of her feelings and words to the fore far beyond the sense of activism and social injustice that inspires much of her work. "Poetry is the language of reconciliation," she explained. "It often reminds us of our better selves and common values. It was that legacy that I really leaned into while writing 'The Hill We Climb,' asking myself 'what can this poem do, here and now, that prose cannot?' There is a specific power in poetry to sanctify, purify and rectify even amidst discord."

At this point in her life, Amanda definitely sees herself on a mission, a personal odyssey to bring poetry out of the dark ages and into a new light of possibility. And like everything else tied to her talent and creative instincts, Amanda is taking that task seriously as she offered in her *Time* interview.

"Poetry is already very cool. Where we run into trouble is when we're looking through such a tight pinhole of what poems can be. We're looking at dead white men. We really need to break out of that pathology that poetry is only owned by certain elites and start highlighting and celebrating poets who reflect humanity in all its colors and breadth."

When contemplating her present and future, Amanda has remained thoughtful and insightful, even on the more well-worn aspects of her life. And beginning way back in the second grade, when a teacher's only semiserious suggestion that the very bright and intuitive second grader run for the highest office in the land someday struck a nerve, Amanda has remained adamantly persistent that she will be the *President of the United States* sometime around 2036. "What's so funny is that people act like I'm joking," she was quoted in a *WGBH News.com* piece. "I'm like I'm dead serious. Why wouldn't I be?"

Obviously there have been doubters who have chalked Amanda's goal up to youthful enthusiasm and bravado. But it is fair to say that in cultivating such high powered, politically savvy relationships as Hillary Clinton, Nancy Pelosi and Michelle Obama, she has begun to build a political team of potential advisors for the long haul. And Amanda has remained insistent that being President some day is definitely on her bucket list. Only now, as she told *People*, it would be a direct path from her words to the White House.

"Now I realize that, perhaps, my path to the presidency might be a different way, that it might be performing my poetry and touching people that way and then entering public office from a platform that was built off of my beliefs, thoughts and ideas."

But as she enters the second half of 2021, her meteoric rise as the first true poetry pop star of the modern era, Amanda seems content to wait out the tides of change in her world that will take her on her next big adventure into a life well lived. When discussing things of a seemingly speculative nature, Amanda has been quick to reflect on a life and career that is, to this point, only scant years in the making as a guidepost to what will come.

"There have been times where I've taken the train, did my makeup and hair in a Starbucks, walked myself to a venue and then performed in front of a thousand people," she reflected in *Time*. "We're always walking this really tentative line of who we are and how the public sees us. I'm handling it a day at a time. I'm learning that 'no' is a complete sentence. And I am reminding myself that this is not a competition.

"It's me following the trajectory of the life that I was meant to lead."

Chapter Sixteen
Amanda Looks at Herself

It seemed almost mystical and poetic that the now 23-year-old Amanda was casting a giant shadow. Whether anyone wanted to admit it or not, Amanda was now an elder statesman. She was at the right place and the right time, watching as her notoriety and the fact that poetry and poets, long something done alone and in shadows, was now hip and, in the last year, had mushroomed into a literal pop culture moment. Amanda, both amazed and bemused, was watching as even younger girls with creative drive and ambition were nipping at her heels, becoming the next generation of national and regional laureates whose words were driven by the promise that Amanda Gorman had become and offered as the baton was showing signs of being passed.

In May, 2021, yet another step was being taken in the evolution of young women and the written word when Alexandra Huynh, an 18-year-old first year student at Stanford University, was named the new National Youth Poet Laureate. And not surprisingly, Alexandra was effusive in a big influence being Amanda as she told *ABC News*. "Her trajectory has changed what I thought was possible for a poet. She has encouraged me to dream big."

Going into May 2021, Amanda has found some semblance of peace in her life.

There is a quiet, contemplative balance away from the world that her fate and her talent have thrust her into. Amanda is at ease with it all. And as she contemplates all that has brought her to this point, she is comfortable with the fact that she is ultimately just the latest in a long line of women who have cultivated the talent to change minds and hearts with the power of her words. Amanda, at the end of the day, is forthright in the fact that she is the one and only Amanda Gorman. But that there will be others coming up behind her to continue the legacy.

"I don't want to become something that becomes a cage," she vehemently told *Vogue*, "where to be a successful Black girl you have to be Amanda Gorman and go to Harvard. I want someone to eventually come along and disrupt the model I have established on fame. I've learned that it's okay to be afraid. And what's more, it's okay to seek greatness."

Chapter Seventeen
Presidential Inaugural Poets

Amanda Gorman's January 21, 2021 inaugural poetry reading was the latest entry in a very exclusive club. So exclusive that, with the inclusion of Amanda, the roster now stands at six. Historically, Presidential Inaugural Poets have had their own moments while the notion has been anything but consistent.

Since the very first Inaugural Poet, all have been at the request of Democratic presidents. No Republicans have ever expressed an interest or desire. And a big reason for the lack of inaugural poets throughout history may well have had something to do with the fact that the vast majority of presidents seem to have been plain, cold spoken men in their speeches and that there was a legitimate fear that their inaugural speeches might have been upstaged by the eloquent poets.

Standard operating procedure for the job is that it is all very last minute from notification to presentation. Poet Richard Blanco, who was Barack Obama's Inaugural Poet in 2013, summed it up rather succinctly in an interview with Boston Public Radio when he said, "They just call you and you have a little bit of time [usually a matter of a few weeks] to put this all together. Every poet sort of creates the snapshot of where the country is at."

Robert Frost - "The Gift Outright" – January 20

Newly elected President John Fitzgerald Kennedy was a cultured, well-educated man. A man who cultivated good books and the power of the written word. And so it came as little surprise that, in November, 1960, he sent a telegram to the reigning icon of poetry, Robert Frost, with the request that he be the first poet to read at a Presidential Inauguration ceremony. Frost, possessed of a pure and witty New England sense of things, responded in kind. "If you can bear at your age the honor of being made President of the United States, I ought to be able at my age to bear the honor of taking some part in your inauguration. I might not be equal to the task but I can accept it for my cause...art, poetry and now, for the first time, taken into the affairs of statesmen."

Kennedy requested that Frost read a family favorite, "The Gift Outright," which was fine with Frost. But the poet became slightly annoyed when Kennedy requested that he change one line from 'Such as she was, such as she would become' to what he considered the more optimistic 'Such as she will become.' Frost, his creative ego firmly in place at age 86, chaffed at the suggested change but ultimately complied. In the meantime, Frost would throw a twist into the plan when, unbeknownst to Kennedy, he composed an original poem entitled "Dedication" that was submitted for approval and accepted as a preamble to "The Gift Outright."

It had been snowing in the days leading up to the inauguration and there was quite a bit of snow on the ground. At the appointed time, Frost began reading "Dedication" but suddenly stopped. The sun's reflection off the snowy ground had made it impossible to read the "Dedication" portion of the poem. He immediately abandoned that part of the poem and read "The Gift Outright" from memory. It was what many considered good, given the circumstances, but not necessarily Frost's finest hour as a live poet. But the next day, *The Washington Post* would set the record straight when its reporting said, "Robert Frost in his natural way stole the hearts of the inauguration crowd."

Maya Angelou – "On the Pulse of Morning" – January 20, 1993

It would be another 32 years before another poet would highlight a Presidential Inauguration ceremony. And when newly inducted President of the United States William Jefferson Clinton broke the poetry draught, he would do it in grand fashion by asking Maya Angelou to participate. Angelou had many years and many poetic words behind her and was considered a genius of pride and passion in the literary world. For Clinton, Angelou would be the perfect choice. But why?

"I knew she got me," declared Clinton in the *American Masters* documentary series. "She understood the times we were living in."

For her part, Angelou in the *New York Times*, agreed that it would make sense. "He understood that I am the kind of person that brings people together. In the *American Masters* documentary, she would reflect

"I was asked if I would consider writing a poem for President Clinton and I said yes."

Almost immediately after agreeing to participate, Angelou was overwhelmed at both the honor of being asked and the pressure that went along with the invitation. "I was overwhelmed," she admitted to the *New York Times* and *American Masters* in separate interviews. "Then I started to pray and began asking the people in the audiences of my speaking engagements to pray for me. I would ask people what they thought I should do? But once I made the decision to do it, I didn't really think about what anybody else said."

Angelou began writing "On the Pulse of Morning" much in the manner she had always done, a ritual stepped in isolation. She rented a hotel room and closeted herself daily from early morning until well into the afternoon, writing down bits and pieces of the poem on legal pads. The theme of the poem was America and Angelou was workmanlike in writing down everything she could think of about the country. "Then it was just a matter of pushing and squeezing it all into a poem."

On the day of the inauguration, Angelou's reading was scheduled to follow President Clinton's acceptance speech. While not an afterthought, there were many who felt that being on after the acceptance speech was a slight to Angelou. Nevertheless, Angelou delivered. With a booming determined voice that has often been described as 'the voice of God,' she turned "On The Pulse Of Morning" into a powerful statement about where the country was and where it was going. Alternately, an exercise in all of Angelou's strengths, "On the Pulse of Morning" was witty and full of wisdom, courage and grace. It was an inaugural poem for the ages and the history books.

But while pundits and historians would rush to put "On the Pulse of The Morning" into perspective, it would be the down home assessment that, in the *American Masters* documentary, would put the day in perspective. "I will always be grateful for her electrifying reading of 'On the Pulse of Morning.'" The poem she wrote and read to us was like all the poems and stories she had ever written. It was a gift," Clinton reflected.

Miller Williams – "Of History and Hope" – January 20, 1997

The massive international response to Maya Angelou's inaugural poem literally dictated that, upon his reelection to the presidency in 1997, President Clinton would once again turn to a poet to set the emotional stage for the next four years. Clinton would look to his Arkansas roots and a well-known regional poet, publisher and teacher named Miller Williams.

Williams and Clinton had known each other since their teaching days at the University of Arkansas in the early 70's. A true Southern gentleman with down home attitudes and a plain spoken eloquence, Williams had prospered on a fairly low key level, authoring more than 25 books while founding the publishing arm of the University of Arkansas. His published work was much in keeping with his life experiences and a philosophy that was very much salt of the earth as he explained during a conversation with *PBS*. "I like to think that the best poetry involves a contest between ordinary conversation and ritual. There is something about the best poem that wants to be set in a pattern like a Gregorian chant and a cocktail party conversation."

What few requirements of the poem that Clinton gave Williams centered around the theme of where the country had gone and where it was going. Williams saw his marching orders for "Of History and Hope" as being very much to his strengths and the importance of the poem from a historical perspective as he acknowledged in a conversation with *Oxford American Magazine*.

"I wanted the poem to be a clear consideration of how a look at the nation's past might help determine where it could be led in the future. I knew that the poem would be listened to by a great many people, reprinted around the country and discussed in a lot of classrooms. So I wanted it to be true, understandable and agreeable."

As Williams stepped to the podium on January 20, 1993, he would be the poetic guide to a country and a people that were in political and social transition and looking for ways to navigate the often choppy waters. Williams, in a reading that lasted a little over four minutes, would prove the ideal choice for this moment in history. Both plain spoken and eloquent, with an emotional and lyrical aside to his familiarity with the world of education and science, Williams both enthralled and enlightened the Washington audience with a reading centered on how people feel coupled with subtle eloquence and a traditional sense of idealism and sense of sincerity, all of which was wrapped up around a challenging question and answer motif that spanned generations of hopes and dreams.

At the end of the day, "Of History and Hope,"

would be poked, prodded and dissected by observers keen on drawing a parallel and/or contradiction to Angelou's "On The Pulse of Morning." The consensus would be that both were equally brilliant in their own way. And, perhaps most importantly, had carried the banner for the tenor of the times.

Elizabeth Alexander – "Praise Song for the Day" – January 2-, 2009

The presidency would be in the hands of the Republicans for the next eight years, coincidentally a time for a hiatus for a poet to make an appearance at an inaugural ceremony. But things would change both historically and, in a sense, for society and equality in 2009 with the election of Barack Obama to the White House. The first Black man to be elected president, Obama brought a young, modern and, to a degree, hip way of thinking to the presidency. And that meant that his inaugural ceremony on January 20, 2009 would bring with it a whole lot of soul, hope and a return to the presence of a poet of stature to the podium.

Obama need not have looked any further than Elizabeth Alexander for the perfect fit. Alexander was a woman, a woman of color and, perhaps most important, a woman of style, grace and distinction on a number of fronts. A multi-tenured professor at such distinguished universities as Yale and George Washington University, Alexander was also the author of several books of poetry, one of which was a Pulitzer Prize finalist, and brought to her creativity a sense of forthrightness and to the point thoughts and messages that made Alexander the ideal poet to anchor the inaugural.

Marc Shapiro

Alexander told *The Washington Post* that she felt that Obama and she were on the same wavelength. "This incoming president of ours has shown in every act that words matter, that words carry meaning and that words are the medium with which we communicate across differences and that words have tremendous possibilities. And that those possibilities are not empty."

While Alexander was honored and thrilled to have Obama pick her, she was realistic enough to concede that the sheer immensity of the situation was not lost on her as she revealed in conversation with National Public Radio. "I did not feel scared but rather challenged." She would further acknowledge to *PBS.org* and the *George Washington University Community Newspaper* that "It's challenging because what you try to do is to both serve the occasion and to find language and imagery that people will want to hold onto after the occasion has passed. What makes the inauguration poem different from a lot of my other work is that it has a job to do. It was chosen for a particular occasion. The best way I can do that is to not give a sermon on the mount but to write something as careful and mindful as I can."

Alexander went about the business of crafting "Praise Song for the Day" in what was, for her, a workmanlike manner with legal pad and pen in hand and, as she offered National Public Radio, thoughts and opportunities at the ready. "I've been trying out phrases and ideas, meditating and looking through scraps of paper I've been noting. It's been a time of tremendous feeling and tremendous thought."

On January 20, 2009, Alexander stepped forward and "Praise Song for the Day" was heard for the first time. "Praise Song for the Day" was every ounce of

108

Alexander and so much more. It was an enticing and, yes, memorable mixture of broad lyrical focus and seemingly small but no less impactful moments brought effectively to the fore. "Praise Song for the Day" was progressive and chance taking. And, as history has no doubt proven, it was a chance worth taking.

Richard Blanco – "One Today" –
January 21, 2013

On first look, Richard Blanco seemed the ideal choice to read "One Today" at President Barack Obama's second inaugural ceremony. He's the classic up from his bootstraps kind of guy. An immigrant and an openly gay immigrant at that. Somebody who has gotten his hands dirty with real workaday work as a civil engineer before rising to a different level as a much-respected poet and speaker. When Blanco speaks it is usually with an enticing mixture of humor, matter of fact tinged with sarcasm. He is plain spoken with the confidence of somebody who has lived it all and seen it all and has arrived at a higher literary calling.

Blanco seemed to Obama the perfect poetic guide to where his second term as president was heading. Blanco would turn self-effacing in a conversation with the *Tampa Bay Times* when, in looking back on his inaugural experience, he deflected his own importance by saying "The poem can say it better than I can."

Fair enough. Blanco's "One Today" is a celebration of the American experience done up in nine stanzas and 69 lines that deftly bring the triumphs of a shared America and its people to the fore with a sense of majesty.

Blanco would be to the point on how it all came to be in an interview with the *Tampa Bay Times*. "The White House asked me to write three poems. They selected one ["One Today"]. Their selection allowed me to do a rewrite which kept the poem similar but which gave me room to make it that much better."

Blanco's creation of "One Today" would take in a lot of research and revisiting the works of old literary friends and influences. He would read a lot of poetry, the likes of Allen Ginsberg, Elizabeth Bishop and, in particular, Nikki Moustakis' poem "How To Write a Poem After September 11." Blanco would also immerse himself in the inaugural poems of Elizabeth Alexander and Maya Angelou.

There was also a less literary helpmate as he recalled in the *Tampa Bay Times*. "I moved my stuff out of my office in my home and worked at the dining room table. There is a view of the mountains that helped me creatively."

But ever the perfectionist, Blanco would find that, after completing a first draft of "One Today," he was not happy with the results. To his way of thinking, something was missing. He spent some time trying to figure it all out. And finally, there was a breakthrough.

"I remembered the lushness of language and texture. The things that I knew about my own background that could speak to others. I went back to that for my voice."

Finally, Blanco had "One Today" where he wanted it. The finished poem was real and not too artsy and not too superior sounding. He felt that it truly represented America and that his creative voice was authentic. Blanco was now confident in his work as he counted down the days to Obama's second inauguration. His memories of that day remain fresh as he wistfully told the *Tampa Bay Times.*

"I was very relieved from all the work I had put in. It was more euphoric than anything else. I was misty eyed. My mother was sitting next to me. I felt a good connection with the crowd. I read "One Today" the way I planned to. I read it at that moment better than I had planned to."

The day remained a bit of a blur. Blanco was congratulated by politicians, people of immense influence and just plain real people. For Blanco it was all good.

Amanda Gorman – "The Hill We Climb" – January 20, 2021

A dark cloud descended on America with the election of Donald Trump. In a Republican world, there was no room for poetry and heartfelt feelings. Tribalism. Overt racism, white supremacy, corruption and an overall picture of a country suddenly not our own had become the order of the day. But on January 20, 2021, the world had suddenly found its senses and taken a turn for the right in humanity and man. And a young black woman with mighty words would lead them back to the garden. You know how she got us here.

Amanda Gorman is the latest in a select line of poets who have shown us the way. She won't be the last.

Chapter Eighteen
Black Women Writers

Amanda Gorman's arrival on the world stage has resulted in a sudden, renewed interest in the lives, history and contributions of black women writers. Names like Maya Angelou, Phillis Wheatley and a handful of others quickly come to mind. But history, dating back as far as slavery in the United States, is replete with some of the earliest and most noteworthy literary contributions by women of color. Thanks to the diligent research of such websites as *Oxford Bibliographies.com*, *Zora.medium.com*, *Thought.com* and *The Tempest.com*, there is a literal panorama of Black women of literary accomplishment to explore.

Phillis Wheatley (1753-1784) holds the distinction of being the first published African American poet. Her book *Poems on Various Subjects Religious and Moral*, published in London in 1773, would become a literary call to arms to the growing anti-slavery movement.

Old Elizabeth (1766-1866) was born into slavery and subsequently sold several times before finally being freed at age 39. In 1863, at age 97, she would write her memoir, *Memoir of Old Elizabeth*: *A Colored Woman* which chronicled her years under slavery.

Maria Stewart (1803-1879) was a freeborn journalist, lecturer and civil rights activist. She was the first woman to speak out publicly on women's rights and was an outspoken civil rights activist. A collection of her lectures would be published by a newspaper called *The Liberator*. For which she would continue to write for years afterward.

Harriet Jacobs (1813-1897) was an author and lecturer who survived brutality and sexual abuse at the hands of white slaveowners before finally escaping to the north where she worked tirelessly for the anti-slavery movement. In 1861, she published her autobiography *Incidents in The Life of a Slave Girl* which chronicled her years of slavery and the mistreatment she endured.

Mary Ann Shad Cary (1823-1893) was the first Black woman to edit and publish a newspaper, the anti-slavery publication *The Provincial Freeman*, a publication devoted to combating slavery. She was also the second Black woman to earn a law degree.

Francis Ellen Watkins Harper (1825-1911) was a poet, author and lecturer. She wrote her first collection of poetry at age 21 and, at that point, made the decision to devote her entire writing life to the anti-slavery movement. Many of her poems, including the most notable *Eliza Harris*, would be published in the abolitionist newspapers *The Liberator* and *North Star*. Her short story *The Two Offers*, published in *Anglo African Magazine*, would give her the distinction of being the first published story by an African American woman.

Charlotte Forten Grimke (1837-1914) was an abolitionist author, poet and educator whose poems, by the late 1850's, were regularly appearing in the anti-slavery newspapers *The Liberator* and *The Evangelist*. Her experiences during the Civil War were recounted in her journals *Life on The Sea Islands* which were published by *The Atlantic Monthly* in 1864.

Lucy Parsons (1853-1942) was a labor organizer, women's rights activist, public speaker and a self-proclaimed anarchist. On December 21, 1886, one of her most powerful and most remembered speeches, "I Am an Anarchist" was published by the *Kansas City Journal*.

Ida Bell Wells Barnett (1862-1931) was a journalist who was not afraid. As the co-owner of the *Memphis Free Speech* newspaper, she was constantly at odds with the white populace because of the anti-racist stance of the paper. When she raised the ire of the whites in town after writing a blistering story condemning the lynching of three Black men, she was forced to leave town after a white mob burned down the *Free Speech* offices. Undaunted, Barnett would continue on, using her investigative journalistic skills, for some of the country's leading newspapers and taking every opportunity to protest racial injustice.

Alice Dunbar Nelson's (1875-1935) first book, *Violets and Other Tales*, was published in 1895. In the ensuing years, her poems, short stories and newspaper columns would take dead aim at racism, Black family life and sexuality.

Angelina Weld Grimke (1880-1958) knew what she railed against and what inspired her. Her short stories and plays drove her opinion that racism in all its forms was abhorrent. Poems such as "The Eyes of My Regret" and "At April and the Closing Door" made regular appearances in the NAACP newspaper

The Crisis and in the anthologies *The New Negro, Caroling Dusk* and *Negro Poets and Their Poems.* Her play *Rachel*, produced in 1920 with an all-Black cast, was one of the first plays to deal with racism.

Georgia Douglas Johnson (1880-1966) was a poet, playwright and was a driving force in the Harlem Renaissance art and literary movement. In 1916, Johnson began publishing her first poems in the NAACP magazine *The Crisis.* From 1926-1932 she wrote a weekly newspaper column called *Homely Philosophy* that appeared in several African American newspapers. During the height of the Harlem Renaissance, Johnson's home would be the regular meeting place of many of the up-and-coming writers who would make a name for themselves in the coming decades. Johnson would go on to become well established in the Black theater community, with the production of several plays during the Harlem Renaissance including productions of *Blue Blood* and *Plumes.*

Jessie Redmon Fauset (1882-1961) was a prolific poet, essayist and reviewer and had the distinction of being the first Black woman to attend Cornell University. She began writing poems and essays for the NAACP magazine *The Crisis* in 1912 before taking over as literary editor for the magazine in 1919.

Anne Spencer (1882-1975) was a Harlem Renaissance poet and activist and the first Black person and Virginian to have her poetry included in the *Norton Anthology of American Poetry.*

Zora Neale Hurston (1891-1960) began her writing life in 1920 with a series of short stories that drew a following in the Black literary community. Her stature would grow in 1930 with the publication of her novel *Mules and Men* and, in 1937, with the critically acclaimed book on the experiences of a Black woman entitled *Their Eyes Were Watching God*. In 1930 Hurston, in collaboration with the writer Langston Hughes, would pen the comedic play *Mule Bone*.

Shirley Graham DuBois (1896-1977) was a prolific playwright whose work focused primarily on the Black experience. Her breakthrough production was the musical drama *Tom Tom* in 1932. She would be at her most prolific in the late 1930's with her plays *Little Black Sambo* and *Swing Mikado*.

Marita Bonner (1898-1971) was the consummate writer of poems and essays who came to prominence during the Harlem Renaissance. Her first published essay "Being Young, a Woman and Colored" appeared in *The Crisis* in 1925. Bonner's short stories would regularly appear in *The Crisis* and *Opportunity* magazines.

Gwendolyn Brooks (1898-1971) was the first Black American to win the Pulitzer Prize for poetry. It was the culmination of a career, to that point, that had already been eventful. At age 13, Brooks first published poem, "Eventide," appeared in *American Childhood Magazine*. By age 17, Brooks' poetry had become a regular feature of *The Chicago Defender* newspaper. Her first collection of poetry, *A Street in Bronzville*, was published in 1945, followed in 1950 by a second volume, *Anne Allen*. Not long after being awarded the Pulitzer Prize, Brooks received another distinguished honor, becoming the first Black woman to be appointed poetry consultant for the Library of Congress.

Margaret Walker (1915-1998) was a poet and novelist. Her book of poetry entitled *For My People* won the Yale Series of Young Poets competition in 1942, making her the first Black woman to win a national writing prize. In 1966, she wrote *Jubilee*, a slavery saga set against the backdrop of the Civil War.

Lorraine Hansberry (1930-1965) was a Black playwright and activist who is best known for her 1959 play *A Raisin in The Sun*. For this effort, Hansberry became the first Black playwright and youngest American to win the coveted New York Critics Circle Award. Of no less note, *A Raisin in The Sun* was also the first Broadway play written by a Black American woman.

Toni Morrison (1931-2019) was a novelist noted for focusing her stories on the Black female experience. Her first book, *The Bluest Eye*, was published in 1973. Morrison's second novel, *Song of Solomon* would follow in 1977 and would result in Morrison receiving the National Book Critics Circle Award. The books and the accolades would keep coming as 1987's *Beloved* would see Morrison become the first Black woman to be awarded the Nobel Prize in Literature.

Audre Lorde (1934-1992) pulled no punches. A self- described "Black, lesbian, feminist mother lover poet," Lorde's work dealt honestly and often in a raw manner with the issues of racism, sexism, classism and homophobia. Lorde published her first poem in *Seventeen Magazine* while still in high school. Her no holds barred style would make the subsequent collections, *Cables to Rage* and *The Black Unicorn*. She would be equally successful when her collection of essays, *Burst of Light*, saw Lorde winning the National Book Award.

Angela Davis (1944) is an author, political

activist and university professor who once captured the spirit of the 60's revolution when she was named to the FBI's Most Wanted list because of her involvement with the Black Panthers. Davis has authored several books on classism, feminism, racism and prison injustice and inequity that include *Women, Race and Class*, *Women Culture and Politics* and *The Meaning of Freedom*.

Alice Walker (1944) is a novelist, poet, essayist and social activist. She published her first novel, *The Third Life of Grange Copeland* in 1970 but would ultimately confirm her literary reputation in 1982 with the publication of *The Color Purple*, for which she would win the Pulitzer Prize for Literature. Walker has been a prolific poet, publishing a number of collections that include *Hard Times Require Furious Dancing*, *Taking the Arrow Out of the Heart* and *Her Blue Body Everything We Know: Earthling Poems*. For her creative efforts, Walker has also been the recipient of the O'Henry Award and the National Book Award.

Bell Hooks (1952) is an author, activist and scholar whose work has helped define relationships between race, gender and social class. She wrote her first book *Ain't I a Woman* at age 19 and, over the years has published literally dozens of books that include *Talking Back: Thinking Feminist, Thinking Black: Black Looks, Race and Representation* and *Where We Stand: Class Matters*.

Ntozake Shange (1948-2018) was a playwright, poet and feminist. She would forever be enshrined in the Black creative hall of fame in 1975 when she wrote the play *For Colored Girls Who Have*

119

Considered Suicide When the Rainbow is Enuf for which she was honored with an Obie Award.

Morgan Parker (1987) is a hybrid poet of sorts whose work combines pop culture references, Black history and her personal life. Her poetry books include *Other People's Comfort Keeps Me Up at Night*, *There Are More Beautiful Things Than Beyonce* and *Magical Negro*.

Jamila Woods (1989) is a poet and singer songwriter. Her poetry has appeared in such publications as *Muzzle*, *Third World Press* and *Poetry*. Songs in her two albums of music, *Heavn* and *Legacy* are all named after notable Black artists.

Aja Monet (1987) is a poet and a community activist. Her first poetry collection is *My Mother Was a Freedom Fighter*.

Maya Angelou (1928-2014) was a poet and a civil rights activist who worked with Martin Luther King, Jr. and Malcolm X during the civil rights movement. Her poetry collection *Just Give Me a Drink of* Cool *Water 'fore I Diiie* was published in 1971 and would be nominated for the Pulitzer Prize the following year. Angelou was awarded the National Medal of Arts in 2000 and the Presidential Medal of Freedom in 2010. Notable of her many published works are *I Know Why the Caged Bird Sings*, *Gather Together in My Name* and *All God's Children Need Travelling Shoes*.

Wanda Coleman (1946-2013) was the author of more than 20 poetry collections focusing on Black poverty, womanhood and racial inequalities in Los Angeles. One of those books, *Mercurochrome*, was a finalist for the National Book Award in 2001.

Lucille Clifton (1936-2019) was featured in the

noted 1970 anthology *The Poetry of The Negro*. Her books *Good Woman: Poems and a Memoir* and *Next: New Poems* were both finalists for the Pulitzer Prize.

Nikki Giovanni (1943) is a poet and children's book author who has been awarded for both her poetry and her activism. She has been the recipient of the Langston Hughes Medal and the NAACP Image Award. Her voluminous bibliography includes *Cotton Candy on a Rainy Day*, *Blues: For All The Changes* and *Quilting The Black Eyed Pea: Poems and Not Quite Poems*.

Tracy K. Smith (1972) was the 22nd Poet Laureate of the United States. She has published more than four collections of poetry including the 2011 Pulitzer Prize winning *Life on Mars*.

Claudia Rankine (1963) books of poetry reflect on violence and aggression against African Americans as well as other aspects of Black life and experience. *Citizen: An American Lyric* being a prime example. That book would be honored with the NAACP Image Award and the National Book Critics Circle Award.

Rita Dove (1952) was the second Black woman to win the Pulitzer Prize in Poetry for her collection *Thomas and Beulah*. Dove's approach to poetry is an effective mix of real life and holding up a literary mirror to racial and social injustices.

Natasha Tretheway (1966) is a mixed-race poet and professor who won the Pulitzer Prize for poetry in 2007 with her collection *Native Guard*.

Sonia Sanchez (1934) has written more than a dozen poetry books during her long and celebrated career. Her book *Does Your House Have Lions?* was nominated for the NAACP Image Award and the

National Book Critics Circle Award. Sanchez was awarded the prestigious Robert Frost Medal for her distinguished contributions and service to American poetry.

Yona Harvey (1974) is a poet, professor and comic book writer. She was the first Black woman to write for Marvel Comics and the author of the book *Hemming the Water* which was a finalist in 2014 Hurston/Wright Legacy Award for poetry.

Eve L. Ewing (1968) is a poet, comic book writer and professor. Ewing is noted for the publication of two poetry collections, *Electric Arches* and *1919* which took a literary and critical look at the Chicago race riots of 1919. She was the writer for the Marvel Comics series *Ironheart* and the author of *Ghosts in The Schoolyard: Racism and School Closures On Chicago's South Side*.

Sources

Magazines

Vice, Harvard Crimson, Time, People, Ten, Black Enterprise, Culture, TLA Magazine, Trek Magazine, Vogue Magazine, Roots Magazine, Harpers Bazaar, S Magazine, Oxford American Magazine,

Newspapers

Harvard Independent, Associated Press, New York Times, Los Angeles Times, Washington Post, The Argonaut, Sacramento Observer, Religion News Service, The Observer, New York Post, George Washington University Community Newspaper,

Websites

Library of Congress.com, Cultural Weekly.com, Girl Boss.com, The Coven Mag.com, Real Black Grandmothers.com, Study Breaks.com, Understood.org, Harvard Gazette.com, California Charter Schools Association.org, Bucknellian.net, The Moth.com, The Project For Women.org, The Project For Women.com, Lily Blog.com, Inspire My Kids.com, The Los Angeles Layolan, USC Annenberg Media.com, LA List.com, Harvard Advocate.com, The Huffington Post.com, Race Relations.com, United Nations Association.org, Warren

Marc Shapiro

Wilson.edu, Vital Voices.org, Discover Gates.org, Ozy.com, Poets And Writers.org, Diverse Education.com, Library Of Congress.gov, Brit&Co.com, The Root.com, Yahoo.com, Cultured Magazine.org, LA Taco.com, IES Abroad.org, Assembly Malala.org, American Sociological Association.org, BBC.com, Vatican News.com, Oxford Biographies.com, Zora. Medium.com, Thought.com, The Tempist.com

Television
KCET, PBS News Hour, Late Night With James Cordon, ABC News, CNN, BBC Breakfast,

Radio
National Public Radio, WGBH news.com, Boston Public Radio,

Miscellaneous
Amanda Gorman's Twitter messages, Interview with Oprah Winfrey, Open Studio with Jared Bown, Mattel Toys website, American Masters

About the Author

New York Times bestselling author Marc Shapiro has written more than 60 nonfiction celebrity biographies, more than 24 comic books, numerous short stories and poetry, and three short-form screenplays. He is also a veteran freelance entertainment journalist.

His young adult book, *JK Rowling: The Wizard Behind Harry Potter,* was on *The New York Times* bestseller list for four straight weeks. His fact-based book *Total Titanic* was also on *The Los Angeles Times* bestseller list for four weeks. *Justin Bieber: The Fever* was on the nationwide Canadian bestseller list for several weeks.

Shapiro has written books on such personalities as Shonda Rhimes, George Harrison, Carlos Santana, Annette Funicello, Lorde, Lindsay Lohan, E.L. James, Jamie Dornan, Dakota Johnson, Adele and countless others. He also co-authored the autobiography of mixed martial arts fighter Tito Ortiz, *This Is Gonna Hurt: The Life of a Mixed Martial Arts Champion.*

He is currently working on group biographies of the Beatle Wives and the Beatle Kids for Riverdale Avenue Books.

Inside Grey's Anatomy: The Unauthorized Biography of Jamie Dornan

Annette Funicello: America's Sweetheart

Game: The Resurrection of Tim Tebow

Lindsay Lohan: Fully Loaded, From Disney to Disaster

Jenni: An Unauthorized Biography

Who Is Katie Holmes? An Unauthorized Biography

Norman Reedus: True Tales of The Waking Dead's Zombie Hunter, An Unauthorized Biography

Welcome to Shondaland: An Unauthorized Biography of Shonda Rhimes

Renaissance Man: The Lin Manuel Miranda Story

John McCain: View from the Hill

www.ingramcontent.com/pod-product-compliance
Lightning Source LLC
Chambersburg PA
CBHW051428090426

42737CB00014B/2863